# The Simple Answer to Using **Windows 95**

This guide has been produced by Sue Rowley and Chris Vaughan, who used to lecture at Wakefield College with special responsibility for resource-based learning in information technology.

© Information Technology Resources 1999

For further copies, please contact us:  Phone: 01977 679221   Fax: 01977 673352
E-mail: help@it-resources.co.uk
www.it-resources.co.uk

Published by:   Information Technology Resources (ITR), Bridgefoot House, Marsh Lane, Beal, East Yorkshire, DN14 0SL.

Printed by:   York Publishing Services, 64 Hallfield Road, Layerthorpe, York, YO3 7XQ.

ISBN 0 9534860 5 2

All rights reserved. You cannot reproduce, store or send any part of this publication without the written permission of the copyright holders.

We have produced certain pages of this book on photocromatic paper. If you attempt to photocopy the page, it will turn the original page black and you will lose all data.

Microsoft® and Windows® are registered trademarks of Microsoft Corporation. All other trademarks are acknowledged as belonging to their respective companies.

# INDEX

*Windows' functions*

**A**

| | |
|---|---|
| A: drive | 13 |
| Accessories | |
|     calculator | 88 |
|     dial-up networking | 89 |
|     fax | 94-97 |
|     imaging | 90 |
|     multimedia | 82, 83 |
|     notepad | 92 |
|     paint | 91, 100 |
|     system tools | 84-87 |
|     wordpad | 93 |
| Add new hardware | 62 |
| Add or remove programs | 63 |
| Add printer | 76 |
| Add program to start menu | 100 |
| Application software | 15 |
| Audio CD | 82, 83 |

**B**

| | |
|---|---|
| Backup | 13, 53, 86 |
|     restore | 87 |
| Bits and bytes | 16 |
| Browse | 17 |
| Buttons on title bar | 26, 37 |
| Buttons on toolbars | 44 |

**C**

| | |
|---|---|
| C: drive - CPU | 13 |
| Calculator | 88 |
| CD ROM drive | 13 |
| Change | |
|     appearance of windows | 67 |
|     desktop icons and colours | 68 |
|     fax cover sheet | 95 |
|     internet settings | 70 |
|     keyboard settings | 71 |
|     mouse setting | 29 |
|     screen saver | 67 |
|     size of window | 27 |
|     way files and folders are shown | 46 |
| Clock | 20 |
|     set date and time | 65, 78 |
| Close | 26 |

Information Technology Resources – User Guide for Windows 95
© ITR 1999

i

**Windows' functions**

# INDEX

**C** (continued)
| | |
|---|---|
| button | 25 |
| window | 26 |
| Windows 95 | 34 |
| Colour settings | 68 |
| Control panel | 60 |
|    accessibility | 61 |
|    add desktop shortcuts | 98 |
|    add new hardware | 62 |
|    add new items to software | 64 |
|    add or remove programs | 63 |
|    add printer | 76 |
|    change desktop background | 66 |
|    fax | 72 |
|    find fast | 60 |
|    fonts | 69 |
|    hardware | 80 |
|    icons | 68 |
|    internet settings | 70 |
|    keyboard settings | 71 |
|    mail and fax | 97 |
|    modem settings | 73 |
|    mouse pointers | 74 |
|    mouse settings | 29 |
|    password settings | 75 |
|    regional settings | 78 |
|    screen saver | 67 |
|    set date and time | 65 |
|    sounds | 79 |
|    startup disk | 63 |
|    windows colour schemes | 67 |
| Computer parts | 5, 6 |
| Copy | |
|    button | 54 |
|    drag | 54 |
|    files and folders | 54, 55 |
|    floppy disk | 50 |
| CPU | 5, 6, 13 |
| Create a new folder | 43 |
| Cursor | 39, 92 |
| Cursor movement keys | 9 |
| Customise - password settings | 75 |

*Windows' functions*

# INDEX

| | |
|---|---|
| **C** (continued) | |
| Cut and paste | 54, 55 |
| **D** | |
| D: drive | |
|    connect to the internet | 105 |
|    install a program | 63 |
|    play audio CD | 82 |
|    record music | 83 |
|    run a program | 102 |
|    volume control | 83 |
| Date and time | 65 |
| Delete | |
|    files or folders | 52 |
|    recycle bin | 30 |
|    temporary files | 53 |
| Desktop | 20 |
|    background | 66 |
|    colours | 68 |
|    icons | 20, 23, 68 |
|    screen saver | 67 |
|    shortcuts | 24, 98, 99 |
|    start button | 20 |
|    taskbar or system tray | 20 |
| Disk defragmenter | 84 |
| Disk drives | 13 |
| Disk space | 81 |
| Downloading | 17 |
| Drag and drop | |
|    boxes | 95 |
|    copy and move files | 54, 55 |
|    icons | 56, 100 |
|    move a window | 26 |
|    my briefcase | 56 |
|    programs to desktop | 98 |
|    programs to start button | 100 |
| DVD ROM | 13 |
| **E** | |
| Electronic mail | 8, 17 |
|    attach files | 110 |
|    e-mail addresses | 109 |
|    internet e-mail | 110 |
|    modems | 8 |

Information Technology Resources – User Guide for Windows 95
© ITR 1999

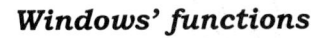

iii

*Windows' functions*

# INDEX

| | |
|---|---|
| **E** (continued) | |
| use address book | 111 |
| **F** | |
| Fax | 72 |
| change fax cover sheet | 95 |
| receive | 97 |
| send | 94 |
| send scanned page | 96 |
| set up computer | 72 |
| Files and folders | 40, 41, 42 |
| backup files | 13, 86 |
| change display | 46 |
| copy | 50, 54 |
| delete | 52, 53 |
| file extensions | 47, 90 |
| find files or folders | 57 |
| find recently used files | 59 |
| icons | 41, 48 |
| move | 55 |
| move from one folder to another | 45 |
| new folders | 43 |
| refresh | 46 |
| rename | 43, 52 |
| save file search | 58 |
| select | 51 |
| share | 104 |
| temporary files | 53 |
| undo rename | 52 |
| Floppy disks | 13, 16 |
| backup | 13, 86 |
| copy | 50 |
| format | 49 |
| virus protection | 18 |
| Fonts | 69 |
| Format a disk | 49 |
| **H** | |
| Hard disk – CPU | 13 |
| Hardware | 5, 6 |
| add new hardware | 62 |
| see hardware on computer | 80 |
| Health protection | 19 |
| Help - contents, index, find | 37 |

*Windows' functions*

# INDEX

| | |
|---|---|
| **H** (continued) | |
| when system stops working | 38 |
| 10 minute tour of Windows | 39 |
| Horizontal scroll bar | 32 |
| **I** | |
| Icons | 23 |
| backup | 86 |
| change | 68 |
| edit and arrange | 99 |
| fax | 97 |
| select | 24 |
| shared | 104 |
| Imaging scan and change images | 90 |
| Install new fonts | 69 |
| Install a program | 63 |
| Internet | 7, 17, 18 |
| change settings | 70 |
| connect | 105, 106 |
| delete internet links | 81 |
| e-mail | 17, 18, 109, 110 |
| e-mail address book | 111 |
| e-mail addresses | 109 |
| ISDN line | 8 |
| ISP | 17, 105-108 |
| modem | 8 |
| search for information | 108 |
| URL | 106 |
| visit web page | 107 |
| **K** | |
| Keyboard | 9 |
| accessibility keys | 61 |
| change settings | 71 |
| shortcut and windows key | 9 |
| windows key | 9 |
| Keyboard shortcuts | 10 |
| **M** | |
| Maximise | 25, 26 |
| all open windows | 36 |
| Memory | 14 |
| Menu Bar | 25 |
| pull down menus | 31 |
| Minimise | 25, 26 |

Information Technology Resources – User Guide for Windows 95
© ITR 1999

v

*Windows' functions*

# INDEX

| | |
|---|---|
| **M** (continued) | |
| all open windows | 36 |
| Modems | 6, 8 |
| ISDN line | 8 |
| settings | 73 |
| Monitor | 5, 6 |
| Mouse | 5, 6, 11 |
| change style of pointer | 74 |
| pointers | 12 |
| setting | 29 |
| Move | |
| between windows | 35 |
| files and folders | 55 |
| from one folder to another | 45 |
| taskbar | 44 |
| toolbar | 44 |
| windows | 26 |
| MS DOS | 15 |
| Multimedia | |
| play CD | 82 |
| record and volume control | 83 |

| | |
|---|---|
| My Briefcase | 56 |
| My Computer | 20 |
| add program to start menu | 100 |
| add shortcuts to desktop | 98 |
| change folder and file display | 46 |
| delete files or folders | 52 |
| files and folders | 41 |
| format a floppy disk | 49 |
| make a copy of a floppy disk | 50 |
| move from one folder to another | 45 |
| see disk space | 81 |
| select files or folders | 51 |
| toolbars | 44 |
| My Documents folder | 40 |
| make a new folder | 43 |
| Networks | 7, 89 |
| **N** | |
| Notepad | 92 |
| Notification area | 20 |
| **O** | |
| Offline | 17, 110 |

vi

Information Technology Resources — User Guide for Windows 95
© ITR 1999

**Windows' functions**

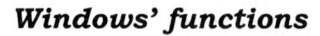

# INDEX

| | |
|---|---|
| **O** (continued) | |
| Online | 17, 110 |
| Open a program | 28 |
|     a program with windows | 101, 102 |
|     a window | 24 |
|     desktop shortcut | 24 |
| Opening screen of Windows | 20 |
| **P** | |
| Paint | |
|     add a program to start menu | 100 |
|     create, scan and change images | 91 |
| Parts of a computer | 5, 6 |
| Parts of a window | 25 |
| Password protect | |
|     internet | 70, 105 |
|     screen saver | 67 |
|     settings | 75 |
| Paste - button | 54, 55 |
| Play a CD | 82, 83 |
| Print | |
|     add a printer | 76 |
|     cancel or pause | 77 |
|     printers | 5, 6 |
|     printer selection | 76 |
|     selected files | 52 |
|     share printers | 104 |
| Programs | |
|     add new items to software | 64 |
|     add or remove | 63 |
|     connect to internet | 105 |
|     open | 28, 92-93, 101, 102 |
|     re-install | 63 |
|     run | 103 |
|     start when windows start | 101, 102 |
| Protection | |
|     password – internet | 70, 105 |
|     password - windows | 67, 75 |
|     virus | 18 |
| Pull down menus | 31 |
| **R** | |
| RAM | 14 |
| Receive a fax | 97 |

*Windows' functions*

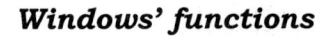

# INDEX

| | |
|---|---|
| **R** (continued) | |
| Recycle Bin | 20, 25 |
|    empty | 30 |
|    open | 24, 30 |
|    restore deleted files | 33 |
| Refresh screen | 46 |
| Regional settings | 78 |
| Re-install programs | 63 |
| Remove programs | 63, 64 |
| Rename files or folders | 52 |
| Restore | |
|    backup files | 87 |
|    button | 26 |
|    deleted files | 33 |
| Run a program | 103 |
| **S** | |
| Scan and change images | 90, 91 |
| ScanDisk | 85 |
| Scanner | 6 |
| Screen saver | 23, 67 |
| Scroll bars | 25, 32 |
| Search for files and folders | 57, 58 |
| Select files | 33, 51 |
| Send a fax | 94, 95 |
| Send e-mail | 109, 110 |
| Send scanned fax | 96 |
| Settings | |
|    control panel | 76 |
|    printers | 76, 77, 104 |
|    taskbar | 100, 101 |
| Share computers | |
|    dial-up networking | 89 |
|    my briefcase | 56 |
|    networks | 7 |
| Share folders and printers | 104 |
| Shortcuts | |
|    on desktop | 24, 98, 99 |
|    keyboard | 10 |
|    key | 9 |
|    right mouse button | 11 |
| Shutdown Windows | 34 |
| Software | 15 |

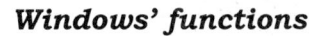

# INDEX

**Windows' functions**

**S** (continued)
| | |
|---|---|
| Sounds | 79 |
| Start button | 20 |
|    open a program | 28, 100 |
| Start Menu | |
|    add a program | 100 |
|    documents | 59 |
|    find files or folders | 57, 58 |
|    help | 37, 39 |
|    programs | 92-95, 97 |
|    run | 103 |
|    settings | 60 |
| Startup disk | 63 |
| Start a program with Windows | |
|    desktop | 101 |
|    taskbar | 102 |
| Status bar | 25 |
| System software | 15 |
| System Tools - backup | 86 |
|    backup restore | 87 |
|    disk defragmenter | 84 |

| | |
|---|---|
| scandisk | 85 |

**T**
| | |
|---|---|
| Taskbar | 20, 26 |
|    load a program | 102 |
|    minimise open windows | 36 |
|    move | 44 |
|    move between windows | 35 |
|    notification area | 20 |
|    settings | 100, 101 |
|    system tray | 20 |
| Temporary files | 53 |
| Ten minute tour of Windows 95 | 39 |
| Time and date | 65, 78 |
| Title bar | 25 |
| Toolbars and tooltips | 44 |

**U**
| | |
|---|---|
| Undo button | 52 |
| Up one level button | 45 |
| User profile | 75 |

**V**
| | |
|---|---|
| Vertical scroll bar | 32 |

*Information Technology Resources – User Guide for Windows 95*
© ITR 1999

**Windows' functions**

# INDEX

**V** (continued)
Visual Display Unit – VDU 5, 6
Virus protection 18
Wallpaper 20, 23, 66, 68, 91
Window 25
    alter size 27
    close, maximise, minimise, restore 26
    change appearance 67
    customise settings 75
    move 26
    open 28
    scroll 32
Windows key 9
Windows desktop 20
Windows Explorer
    add shortcuts to desktop 98
    change files and folders display 46
    copy files and folders 54
    delete files or folders 52
    delete temporary files 53
    file types and icons 48
    files and folders 42
    format a floppy disk 49
    make a copy of a floppy disk 50
    make a new folder 43
    move from one folder to another 45
    rename files and folders 52
    select files or folders 51
    share folders 104
    show file extensions, hidden files 47
    toolbars 44
    undo rename 52
    update files using My Briefcase 56
Windows messaging 97
Windows 95 opening screen 20
WinZip 47
WordPad 93
Word wrap 92
World Wide Web 7, 17, 106, 107, 108

**Z**
Zip drive 13

*Computer basics*

# Welcome to The Simple Answer To Using Windows 95

**This is a very valuable resource if you are:**

- the new owner of a computer;
- a new user of Windows;
- using Windows at home;
- using Windows at work;
- following a programme of study at school, college or university;
- an extensive user, and you have taught yourself; or
- an infrequent user.

This simple, easy-to-follow reference guide will support your needs at home, in the workplace and throughout your programme of study.

*Computer basics*

## The Simple Answer to using Windows 95

### This guide aims to:

- help **you** use Windows through a simple, relevant, practical, guided approach;
- increase your confidence when using Windows;
- help you to use the hardware and software correctly and efficiently;
- provide information and support as and when **you** need it;
- provide a simple, quick, reference guide on how to use the different features and techniques of Windows;
- show you how to customise your computer using the Windows' features and options;
- help you get connected to the internet;
- show you how to send and receive faxes and e-mails.

*Computer basics*

# How do I ...?

## Use this guide

We introduce the features of Windows through the question 'How do I ...?' followed by a simple, concise guide on how to carry out the function.

In this guide we present the range of options available to carry out a specific function. We present options in the following order: 'icon or button' 📋 , keyboard shortcut keys, for example, **'Ctrl C'** (**hold down** the Control key and **press 'C'**); or 'pull down' menu. Instructions such as **'Edit, 'Copy'** mean **pull down** the **'Edit'** menu and **click** on the **'Copy'** option. The 'shortcut menu' available by clicking the right mouse button is also shown.

Bold text means you should take action, in other words press a button on the computer or observation, for example, using a window.

A down arrow at the side of a box shows there are further options. **Click** on this to reveal the list.

*Computer basics*

## Quick reference section

We have included information on computer basics such as hardware and software, networks, modems, keyboard layout, using the mouse, disk drives, bits and bytes, the internet, virus and health protection, windows and much more that you will find useful as an introduction.

Throughout the guide, we have included pictures of the screen to give you an idea of what will happen on screen.

*Computer basics*

## Parts of the computer

'Anything you can touch' is called 'hardware'. The computer is made up of the following hardware. All the parts are connected into the Central Processing Unit with cables.

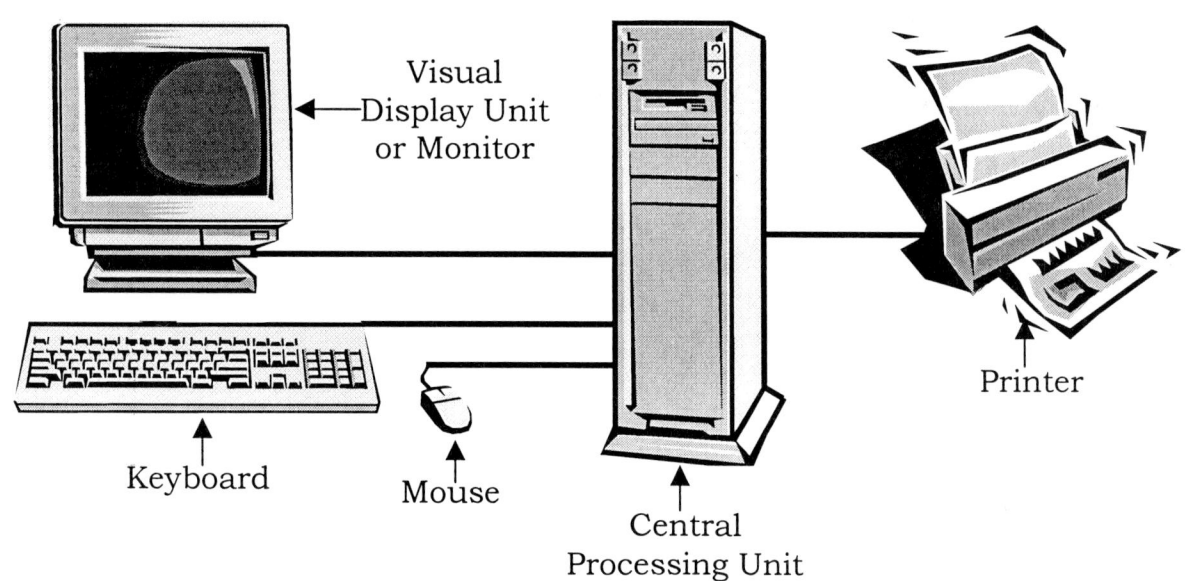

Visual Display Unit or Monitor

Keyboard

Mouse

Central Processing Unit

Printer

Information Technology Resources – User Guide for Windows 95
© ITR 1999

*Computer basics*

## **Hardware**

The parts of a computer are shown on page 5. Yours may look different, but will probably include the same basic parts, though you may have other hardware such as a scanner, digital camera, zip drive, external modem (see page 8) or external speakers.

A scanner is used to read pictures directly into your computer; a digital camera stores photographs in a format which can be used on the computer; a zip drive allows you to store large amounts of data on a disk which can be used on other computers and speakers can either be included in your monitor or stand on your desk.

The Central Processing Unit (CPU) is the computer with all the other items – called 'peripherals' - connected to it by cables. The screen is called the 'visual display unit' (VDU) or 'monitor' and is usually in colour. The keyboard (see page 9) is used to 'input' data onto the screen. The mouse is used to open menus and access buttons, drag files for moving or copying and to position the cursor which shows where anything you key-in will appear on the screen. The printer is used to 'output' the work from the computer. Laser printers will give high quality text and pictures, usually in black and white. Inkjet printers are used for colour printing.

*Computer basics*

## Networks

If you are using a computer at work, you may be part of a network. Networks connect computers together so that they can 'talk' to each other. They also allow users to share folders, printers (see page 104) and 'software'. There are 2 types of network, Local Area Networks (LANs) and Wide Area Networks (WANs).

Local area networks usually operate within the same building. Computers are connected with cables and usually share 'resources' such as printers or a scanner. In a wide area network, machines are connected through either the telephone lines, leased lines with direct access or wire-less technologies. This gives access to other computers over a wide area.

The internet is a collection of networks all linked together which allows computer users to talk to other users all over the world. The world wide web is only part of the internet (see page 17). It is very 'user-friendly' and lets you get into and search through the mountain of information stored on the internet.

*Computer basics*

## Modems

You need a modem to send e-mail which means electronic mail, (see page 110) and faxes (see page 94) directly from your computer or to use the internet.

Modem is short for **mo**dulator-**dem**odulator. If you want to send a message from your computer, it goes through the telephone lines. However, a computer stores information in 'digital' format and telephones use 'analogue' signals. A modem in your computer will change the digital signals from your machine into analogue signals, which can go down the telephone lines. When it reaches the computer at the other end, the modem in that machine will change the signals back into digital format so that it can be read. An ISDN (Integrated Services Digital Network) line can be used which moves information much faster down the telephone lines, but you will need an ISDN modem to use with this.

You can have a modem inside your computer (internal) or one plugged in to the back of your computer (external). With an internal modem, the telephone cable plugs into the back of the computer, whereas with an external modem it connects to the modem itself. Some modems can also be used as answering machines for your telephone and some memory modems work even when your computer is switched off.

*Computer basics*

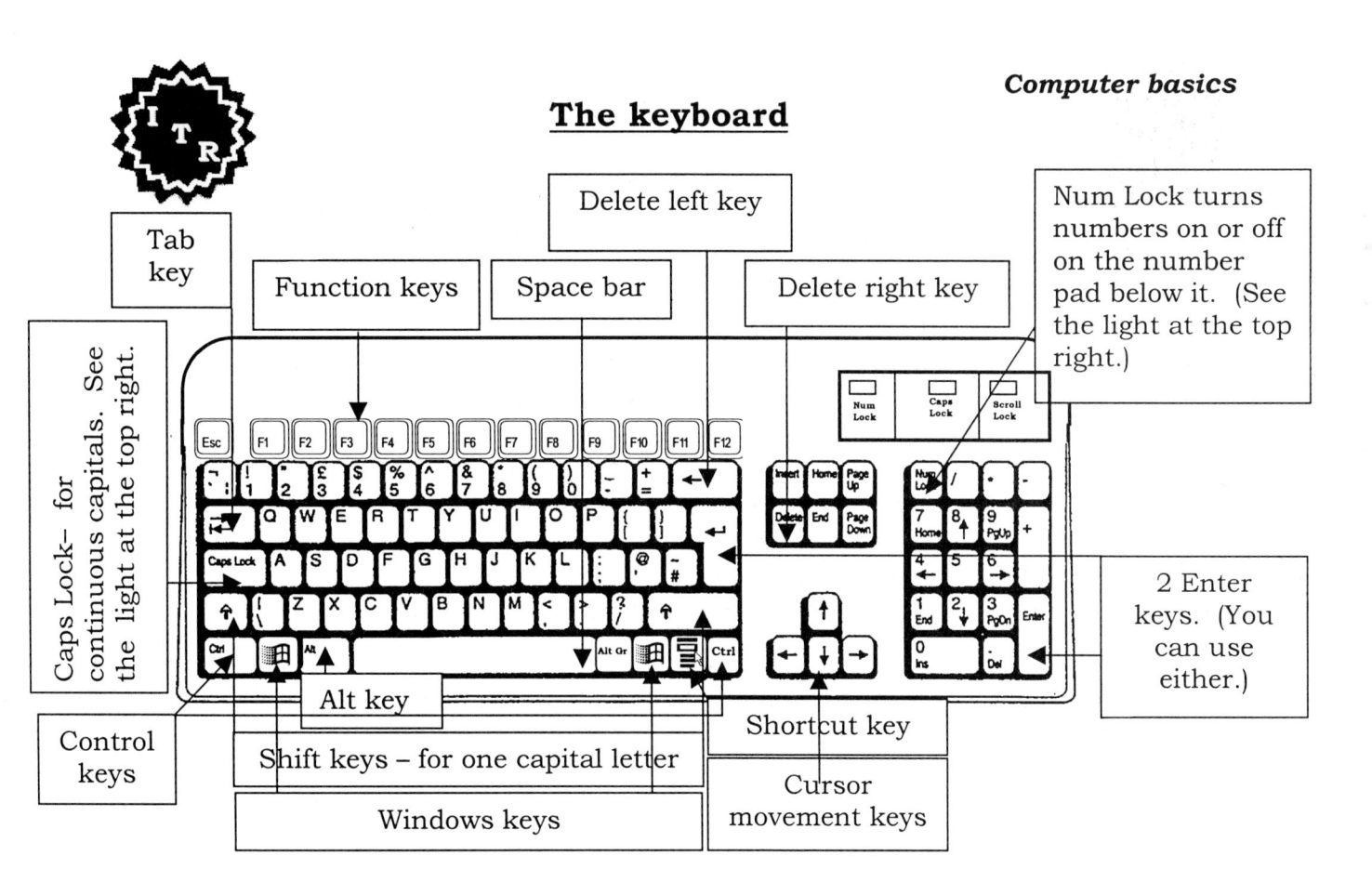

# The keyboard

- Delete left key
- Tab key
- Function keys
- Space bar
- Delete right key
- Num Lock turns numbers on or off on the number pad below it. (See the light at the top right.)
- Caps Lock – for continuous capitals. See the light at the top right.
- 2 Enter keys. (You can use either.)
- Control keys
- Alt key
- Shift keys – for one capital letter
- Windows keys
- Shortcut key
- Cursor movement keys

Information Technology Resources – User Guide for Windows 95
© ITR 1999

*Computer basics*

## Keyboard shortcuts

You can use the keyboard rather than 'menus' or 'toolbars'. **Hold down** the 'Control', 'Shift', 'Alt' or 'Windows' key if shown (see page 9), and **press** the next key.

| | | | |
|---|---|---|---|
| Close a folder and those attached to it | Shift Close | Open 'Run' window | Windows R |
| Copy | Ctrl C | Open Windows Explorer | Windows E |
| Copy a file | Ctrl + drag | Paste | Ctrl V |
| Create a shortcut | Ctrl Shift + drag | Quit a program | Alt F4 |
| Cut | Ctrl X | Refresh a window | F5 |
| Delete | Delete | Rename an item | F2 |
| Delete without using Recycle Bin | Shift Delete | See item properties | Alt Enter |
| Esc | Leave a menu | See the 'Start' menu | Windows key |
| Find a folder or file | Windows F | See the folder one level up | Backspace |
| Help | F1 | See the shortcut menu | Shortcut key |
| Minimize all windows | Windows M | Select all | Ctrl A |
| Move through open windows | Alt tab | Undo | Ctrl Z |
| Move through options in a window | Tab | Undo minimise all windows | Shift Windows M |

*Computer basics*

## The mouse

The mouse is a pointing device plugged into the computer or, on a portable computer it can be part of the keyboard. Move the mouse in any direction and the pointer moves on screen. You will use the left mouse button in most circumstances. There are 4 functions.

- **Pointing** – placing the mouse pointer over an item.
- **Clicking** – pressing and releasing the left button.
- **Double clicking** – tapping the left button twice rapidly and releasing (see page 24).
- **Dragging** – clicking and holding down the left button while moving the mouse pointer.

In Windows you will use the right mouse button to display the 'shortcut menu'. This menu will have different choices depending upon what you are pointing the mouse at when you click.

If you are left-handed, you can reset the mouse to use the right button instead of the left (see page 29).

*Computer basics*

## Mouse pointers

These are the mouse pointers used in Windows 95, you can change them if you want to (see page 74).

**Normal select** – used when you point to objects

**Help select** – found when you click on ? in a window

**Working in background** – means you can still work

**Busy** – means wait until this cursor disappears

**Crosshair cursor** – used when drawing frames

**I-beam cursor** – found when pointer is over text

**Handwriting cursor**

**Not available** – click inside a window

**Vertical size** – changes the height of a window

**Horizontal size** – changes the width of a window

**Diagonal size 1** – changes height and width of a window

**Diagonal size 2** – as above, but in a different direction

**Move** – pick up and move an object

**Alternate select**

Information Technology Resources – User Guide for Windows 95
© ITR 1999

*Computer basics*

## **Disk drives**

Computers have several disk drives, identified by letters of the alphabet followed by a colon (:). Inside the CPU (see page 6) is a fixed, hard disk, which is known as 'drive c:'. This is usually very large and stores gigabytes of data (see page 16). Some hard disks are divided into smaller areas or drives, this is called 'partitioning' and changes the letter used for the CD ROM drive. The other drives are as follows.

Drive A: The floppy disk drive. Data stored on a floppy disk can be moved between machines. Useful for making back-up copies of data (see page 86). Lock these disks away to keep the data secure.

Drive D: The CD ROM drive, which stands for 'Compact Disc Read Only Memory'. CD ROMs hold vast amounts of information. Some computers can write information onto a CD. Others have a DVD ROM drive which means 'Digital Versatile Disc' and can hold much more than a CD ROM.

A 'zip' drive is a portable, external drive which can store up to 250 Mb of data on a disk similar to, but much larger than, a floppy disk. If you are working on a network, you may have lots of other 'drives' you can use. These are sections of the network identified with different letters of the alphabet.

**Computer basics**

## Memory

You can save files onto the hard drive and they will stay there until you delete them. However, there is another type of memory in the computer called the RAM memory, this stands for Random Access Memory. Things stored in the RAM will be lost when the machine is turned off. The computer uses this type of memory when it loads 'application software' (see page 15). When you have work on the screen it is only held in the RAM memory, so if you turn the machine off you will lose the data. You must save data to a disk before it is secure. You may find that your computer stops working when you still have work on screen which you have not been able to save (see page 38).

The RAM memory stores data on 'chips', tiny pieces of hardware which sit inside the machine. The amount of RAM memory your computer has is important. Most computers have at least 32 Mb (see page 16) of RAM, though you would find at least 96 Mb in a new computer and sometimes much more. The more RAM memory your computer has, the easier and faster it is to run more 'application software' programs (see page 15) at the same time.

*Computer basics*

## Software

Software is 'anything you cannot touch', this means the programs that run the computer. There are 2 types of software as shown below.

- System software –Windows 95 the program that loads when you switch on your machine. This shows **'MS DOS'**, **'M**icro**s**oft **D**isk **O**perating **S**ystem', as lots of different windows which make it easier to use. Windows works in the background all the time the computer is on and runs other programs for you and links all the hardware together and makes it work. It is used for creating, moving, copying and deleting files and folders (see pages 43, 55, 54 and 52). It is called 'Windows' because everything you do is inside a window, you can open lots of windows at the same time and bring the one to the front that you want to work on (see page 35).
- Application software – these are programs that you load alongside the system software, which also use windows on screen. You would load WORD 97 for word processing tasks such as writing letters, memos and reports; EXCEL 97 for producing spreadsheets where numbers and calculations are needed and ACCESS 97 for databases, where you want to keep records of names and addresses. You can transfer data from one 'application' to another very easily when you are running Windows.

*Computer basics*

## Bits and bytes

Data is stored in a computer in a digital format either as 1's or 0's. The smallest unit that can be stored is called a 'bit'. Eight 'bits' make up a 'byte'. Think of a 'byte' as being one character, which could be a letter, number, punctuation mark, special sign or space.

A 'kilobyte' or 'Kb' is equal to 1000 'bytes' or, exactly 1024 bytes.

A 'megabyte' or 'Mb' is equal to 1000 'kilobytes' or, exactly 1024 kilobytes.

A 'gigabyte' or 'Gb' is equal to 1000 'megabytes' or, exactly 1024 megabytes.

Floppy disks can hold from 1.44 Mb up to 120 Mb. Hard drives (drive c:) can store anything up to 17 Gb and 'zip' drives up to 250 Mb, but they will all be able to store more and more as time goes by.

```
1 byte  =   one character
1 Kb    =   1000 (one thousand) bytes
1 Mb    =   1,000,000 (one million) bytes
1 Gb    =   1,000,000,000 (one billion) bytes
```

*Computer basics*

## The internet

To be able to use the internet you will need a 'modem' (see page 8) and an 'ISP' which means 'Internet Service Provider'. Many ISP's such as 'Freeserve' are now free. You have to load their 'application software' onto your computer.

The internet is made up of different networks around the world all joined together. When you connect to the internet, you can get information from computers in many different countries. The World Wide Web (www) is only part of the internet and holds lots of information on 'web pages'. You can 'browse', this means look through, these pages. You can copy files from the web onto your computer, called 'downloading', or buy goods and services.

The internet is used to send 'electronic mail' called 'e-mail' (see page 110). You can send a message, with pictures and photographs, just like a letter, but the address it is going to is the electronic address of a computer. 'E-mail' waits in an 'electronic pigeonhole' until the person using the computer reads it. This is a very quick and easy way to send messages. However, as it uses your telephone line it can be costly and others cannot make telephone calls. Write your message in WORD 97 or WordPad first, this is working 'offline' and then connect to the internet and copy it onto your e-mail message when you are 'online'.

**Computer basics**

## Virus protection

Viruses spread among computers like cold germs amongst people. They can come from using other people's floppy disks in your computer, from files which are downloaded from the internet or from e-mail messages you receive. It is recommended that everyone runs a virus protection program on their computer. This runs all the time the computer is switched on and tells you if your machine has been infected.

There are many good protection systems on the market, see your local software supplier for a copy. Most allow you to update your computer protection on a regular basis, either from the internet or from CD ROM. They will also create a floppy disk which will start your computer in an emergency.

It is good practice to scan any floppy disks that have been used on another computer before you use them on your own machine. If a virus does attack your computer, the virus scan program will identify it for you and kill the virus. If it cannot kill the virus, it will tell you which files to delete to get rid of it.

More than 200 new viruses appear every month, and it is essential that you keep your virus scan system up-to-date.

*Computer basics*

## Health protection

It is important to think carefully about how you arrange your computer working space, called 'ergonomics'. You should always avoid having food and drink near your machine and also try to do the following:

- sit in a chair which will adjust so that your back is supported;
- keep your feet flat on the floor;
- place the screen so that light is not shining directly onto it;
- try an anti-glare screen to cover the monitor to prevent eyestrain and headaches;
- make sure the monitor is at a suitable height so that your neck is not at the wrong angle;
- keep the monitor directly in front of you;
- use wrist pads to keep your arms at a comfortable angle, or rest your wrists on the desk in front of the keyboard;
- take breaks quite often.

If you are working on your machine for long periods, it is in your own interests to make sure that you follow these guidelines.

*Computer basics*

## The 'desktop' – the opening screen of Windows

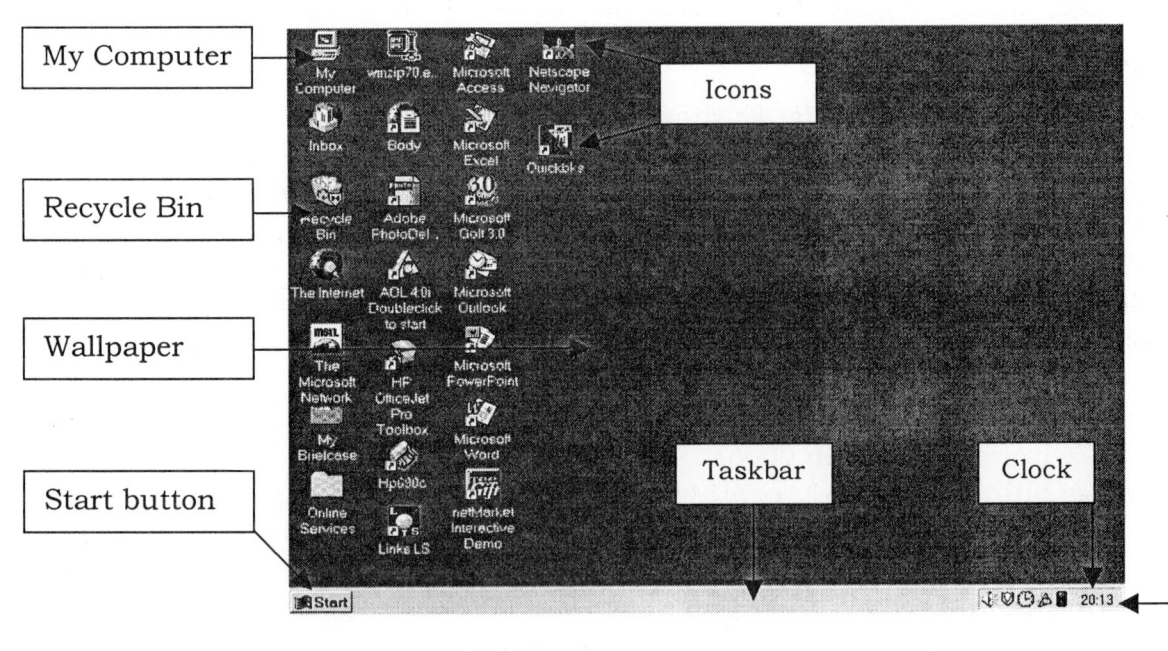

- My Computer
- Recycle Bin
- Wallpaper
- Start button
- Icons
- Taskbar
- Clock
- Notification area or System tray

Information Technology Resources – User Guide for Windows 95
© ITR 1999

**Computer basics**

## Windows 95 section

This section introduces the functions that you will use. We present the information in an easy-to-follow format, including how to:

- Switch programs using the taskbar;
- Copy, move, delete and find files and folders;
- Change the desktop and settings;
- Add and remove programs;
- Send and receive faxes;
- Install a new printer;
- Play sounds and music on your computer;
- Make backup copies of important data;
- Stop documents printing;
- Scan and change images;
- Use the Paint program;
- Add shortcuts to your desktop;
- Start programs when you load Windows;
- Use the internet;
- Send e-mails;
- Shortcuts.

Keep the guide handy for quick reference on both new and previously-used functions. Throughout the section we have included pictures of the screen to give you an idea of what will happen next (see page 22).

*Computer basics*

## **Screenshots**

Throughout this book, screenshots have been included to help you see how the screen will appear when you take an action.

However, the software that you have installed on your computer will make everyone's screenshots look slightly different. Also, when Windows is loaded it does not include all the features in its 'Typical' installation. This is the one most likely to have been chosen if Windows is already running on your computer.

In some cases, the options you want may not be available on your machine. You can choose to add further features to your Windows' installation, if you have space on your hard drive (see page 81).

Always make a note of the original settings before making any changes, so that you can go back to them should you wish to.

*Windows' functions*

## How do I ...?

### Load Windows 95

**Switch** on the external modem (if you have one), **switch** on your computer at the CPU (see page 6) and any other hardware such as speakers, printer or scanner. A short program runs which checks the different parts of the computer.

The Windows operating system will then load to this opening screen, called the Windows' 'desktop'. Yours may look different, but everyone will have 'My Computer', 'Recycle Bin' and the 'Start' button. The pictures are called 'Icons' (see page 20) and they are shortcuts to the programs you use the most, therefore the more 'application software' (see page 15) you have loaded on your computer the more 'icons' you could have on your 'desktop'. You can set these up yourself (see page 98).

Windows has certain settings which always apply unless you change them. These include 'screen savers' (see page 67) and 'wallpaper' (see page 66).

*Windows' functions*

## How do I ...?

### Open a 'desktop' shortcut

'Icons' or pictures on your 'desktop' are shortcuts which open the 'application software' (see page 15) that you use the most or a Windows' 95 function. **Double click** (see page 11) on the picture above the 'Recycle Bin' to open its 'window'.

Or, you can **click** once on the icon and it is 'selected', that is it turns blue. **Press 'Enter'** to open the 'window'.

A double click means you are doing 2 things at the same time. So when you double click on an 'icon' it does the same thing as when you click on it once and press 'Enter'. You will use this double click a lot, so practise until you can do it. If you have difficulty with the double click, try resetting its speed (see page 29).

You can add your own 'shortcuts' to the 'desktop' (see page 98).

*Windows' functions*

# How do I ...?

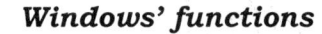

## **Recognise the parts of a window**

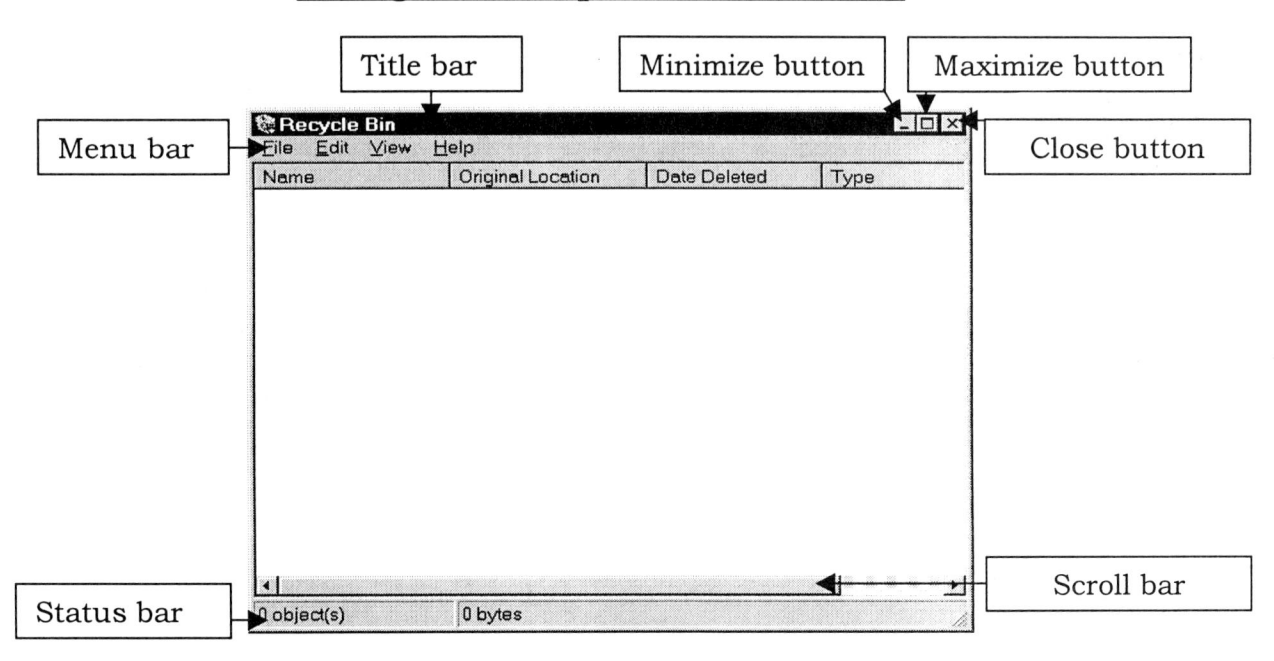

Diagram labels: Title bar, Minimize button, Maximize button, Menu bar, Close button, Status bar, Scroll bar

Recycle Bin window showing:
- File Edit View Help
- Columns: Name | Original Location | Date Deleted | Type
- 0 object(s) | 0 bytes

*Windows' functions*

## How do I ...?

### Minimize, maximize, move and close windows

At the right of the 'title bar' (see page 25) there are 3 buttons [_ □ X] for changing the size of the window.

**Click** on the 'Minimize' [_] button and 'Recycle Bin' is shrunk on to the 'taskbar' (see page 20) at the bottom of the screen. The 'taskbar' displays the 'Recycle Bin' icon. **Click** on the icon or name to show the window again.

**Click** on the 'Maximize' [□] button to change to a full screen. The middle button then changes to the 'Restore' [🗗] button. **Click** on this to change the display back to one small window and the 'desktop'. Wherever you have 2 windows (not the 'desktop') on screen, **click** on any part of the back window to bring it to the front. The window with the blue 'title bar' is the 'active' window you are using.

To move a window, **click** on the 'title bar' and **drag** (see page 11) the window to a new position.

**Click** on the 'Close' [X] button to exit (leave) the window.

*Windows' functions*

## How do I ...?

### Change the size of a window

Windows can appear anywhere on the screen and you may have to move them to see what is behind them (see page 26).  Or, you can alter the size of the window.

**Point** the mouse at the border around the window and the pointer changes from to a ↕ on the top and bottom, a ↔ on the sides and a ↖ when you point at the corners.  When the pointer changes, **click** and **hold down** the left mouse button and **drag** the border to make the window a different size.

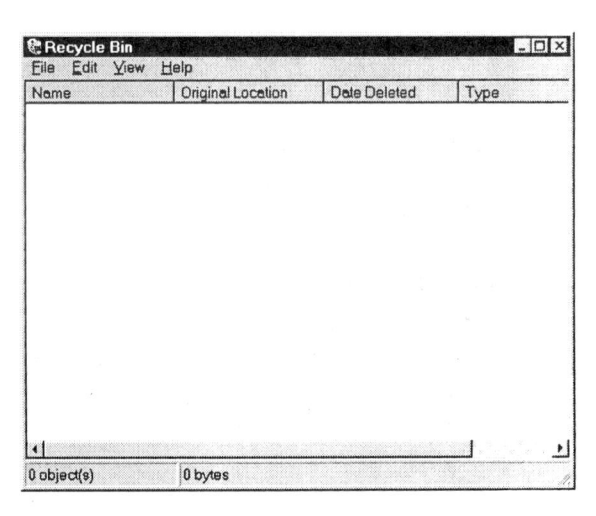

If you point at a corner to re-size the window, it will change both the height and width of the window at the same time.

*Windows' functions*

# How do I ...?

## Open a program using the Start button

If you do not have a 'shortcut' on the desktop for a program, you can run it using the 'Start' button.  **Click** on the 'Start' [Start] button or **press** the 'windows' key on the keyboard.

This 'pop-up' menu will appear; yours may look a little different.  Use the mouse to **move** the 'highlight bar' and **position** it on 'Programs'. Next to 'Programs' is a ▶, this means that when you choose this option a further menu will be shown.  Keep the 'highlight bar' steady on 'Programs' and a list of those available is shown.  **Move** across onto the new menu and **click** on the program you want to open.  Or, instead of the mouse, you can use the 'cursor movement keys' (see page 9).  The ↓ will move the 'highlight bar' from the top of the 'Start' menu down, use the ↑ and it starts at the bottom and moves up, **press** → to show the list of programs.  Use ↓ or → (you may have to press this more than once) to **position** the 'highlight bar' over the one you want and **press 'Enter'** to open the program.  Some programs have a second list of options available, choose these in the same way.  Use ← or **press 'Esc'** to move back through the menus and close the 'Start' menu.

28  Information Technology Resources – User Guide for Windows 95
© ITR 1999

*Windows' functions*

## How do I ...?

### Change the mouse setting

The mouse is set for a right-handed person to use the first finger of the right hand to click the left mouse button. If you need to change the setting to click the right mouse button with the first finger of your left hand, do this as follows.

**Click** on the 'Start' button or **press** the 'windows' key on the keyboard. **Click** on **'Settings'**, **'Control Panel'**, and **double click** on the **'Mouse'** icon to show this second window. **Click** on **'Left-handed'** under 'Button configuration' and **click** on **'Apply'** with the left mouse button. You can also change the speed of the double click. **Click** and **drag** the speed indicator to the left and then **double click** on the **'Test area'** to try out your new setting. When the jack-in-a-box appears the new speed has been recognised by Windows, **double click** on the jack-in-a-box to remove him and try again if needed, **click** on **'OK'**. If you cannot use the mouse you can use the 'cursor movement keys' (see page 9).

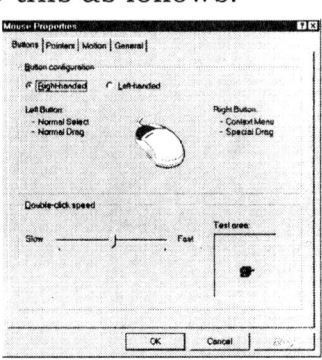

Information Technology Resources – User Guide for Windows 95
© ITR 1999

29

*Windows' functions*

# How do I ...?

## Use the Recycle Bin

The 'Recycle Bin' is Windows' wastepaper basket.  When you delete a file, it goes into the recycle bin, though this may not happen if you are working on a network.  Deleted files are stored in the bin and can be 'restored' back to where they came from.

Just like your wastepaper basket, the 'Recycle Bin' becomes full and needs to be emptied, or it takes up space on your computer.  Deleted files are shown as pieces of paper inside the bin.  This icon displays an empty bin.  Once it has been emptied, files can no longer be restored and are permanently deleted.

At the 'desktop', **double click** on the picture above **'Recycle Bin'**, or you can **click** on it once and **press 'Enter'** to show this window.   **Click** on the **'File'** menu (see page 31) for the option to **'Empty Recycle Bin'**.  If you have nothing in 'Recycle Bin' this item will be 'greyed-out', otherwise **click** on it and you will be asked if you are sure you want to remove the files. **Click** on **'Yes'**.

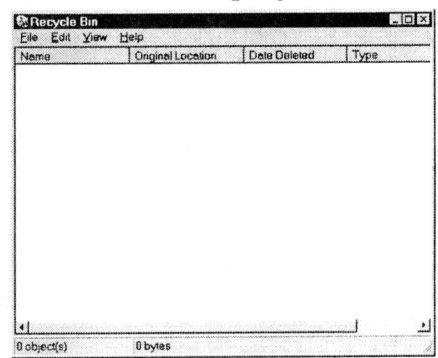

30     Information Technology Resources – User Guide for Windows 95
© ITR 1999

*Windows' functions*

# How do I ...?

## Use pull-down menus

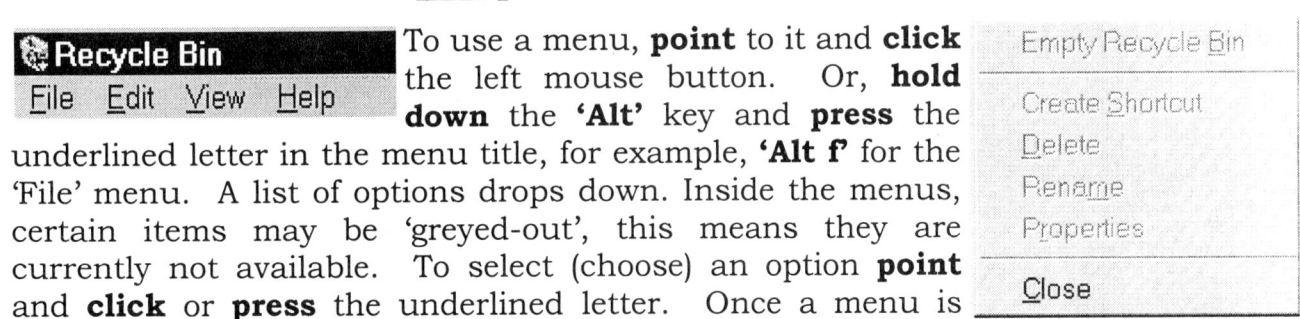

To use a menu, **point** to it and **click** the left mouse button. Or, **hold down** the **'Alt'** key and **press** the underlined letter in the menu title, for example, **'Alt f'** for the 'File' menu. A list of options drops down. Inside the menus, certain items may be 'greyed-out', this means they are currently not available. To select (choose) an option **point** and **click** or **press** the underlined letter. Once a menu is open, move the mouse left or right through the menu bar to open others. To close a menu without making a choice, **click** anywhere outside it.

You can select items without using the menus if you know the 'keyboard shortcuts' which are shown in the menus. **Pull down** the **'Edit'** menu and it tells you to **hold down** the 'Ctrl' key and **press a** to 'Select All'. You can only do this outside the menu. In the **'View'** menu, a tick alongside an item shows it is 'selected', **click** to remove the tick. A dot by an item shows that item in its group is chosen. **Click** on another group member to change the selection. A ▶ shows there is a further menu.

*Windows' functions*

# How do I ...?

## Scroll through a window

If a window like the 'Recycle Bin' has a list of files which is longer or wider than the window, 'scroll bars' appear at the side and bottom of the screen. You can use these or the 'cursor movement keys' (see page 9) to move through the list of files.

The 'vertical scroll bar' is at the right of the window.  **Click** on the ▲ to move towards the top of the list.  **Click** on the ▼ to move towards the bottom of the list.  Or, you can use the ↑ or ↓ on the keyboard to move through the list.

**Click** and **drag** the elevator (the grey lozenge) to move quickly through your files.

**Click** anywhere on the scroll bar above the lozenge to move up one screen and below the lozenge to move down one screen.  The 'horizontal scroll bar' is at the bottom of the screen and works in the same way.  Or, use the ← and → to move through the columns.

*Windows' functions*

## How do I ...?

### Restore deleted files

Deleted files which are still in the 'Recycle Bin' can be 'restored' to where they came from.  **Open** the 'Recycle Bin' and you are shown a list of files.  To select just one file **click** on it and it turns blue.  To select more than one file **hold down** the 'Ctrl' key and **click** on the files you want to restore.  To select several files which are listed together, **click** on the first one, **hold down** the 'Shift' key and **click** on the last one.  All the files between the 2 clicks will be selected.

When the files are selected, **click** on the **'File'** menu and you will see a new option, 'Restore', is now shown.  **Click** on **'Restore'** to put the files back in the place that they came from.

If you have deleted a folder (see page 52) only the files it contained, not the folder, will be seen in 'Recycle Bin'.  However, if you decide to restore them, Windows will create the folder again and put them in it.  This happens even if you only restore one file and not all the files in the folder.

*Windows' functions*

## How do I ...?

### Close down Windows

You must be careful to close down Windows in the proper way. If you do not then you risk corrupting, that is damaging, some of the Windows' files.

**Close** all open windows using the 'Close' button or you can **hold down** the **'Alt'** key and **press F4** (this is function key marked F4 at the top of the keyboard).

**Click** on the 'Start' button or, **press** the 'windows' key and **click** on **'Shut Down'**. The 'Shut Down Windows' window is shown on screen. Read all the options, they may be slightly different on some computers. 'Shut down the computer?' has a black mark alongside it and a box round it. This is the selected item.
**Click** on **'Yes'** and wait for a message to tell you it is safe to turn off the computer. Some machines may switch off automatically.

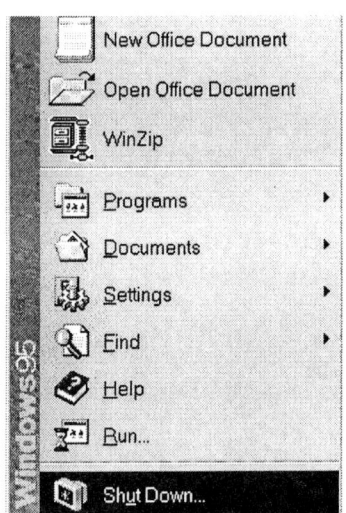

34    Information Technology Resources – User Guide for Windows 95
© ITR 1999

*Windows' functions*

# How do I ...?

## Move between windows

Windows can open lots of 'application software' (see page 15) at the same time, but it may slow down the computer, the speed depends upon the size of your computer's memory.

**Press** the 'windows' ⊞ key or **click** on **'Start'**, **'Programs'**, **'Accessories'** and **'WordPad'** to open Windows' word processing program. **Click** on the 'Maximize' button (see page 26) if needed. **Click** on **'Start'**, **'Programs'**, **'Accessories'** and **'Calculator'** to open the calculator in front of WordPad. The 'title bar' on WordPad is now greyed-out and on the 'Calculator' it is blue, showing this is the 'active' window. **Click** on the 'Minimize' button on 'Calculator' to shrink it down onto the 'taskbar'. **Minimize** 'WordPad' in the same way. You are now at the 'desktop' with 'Document – WordPad' and 'Calculator' showing on the 'taskbar'. **Open** the 'Recycle Bin' (see page 30). The 'taskbar' looks like this. **Click** on each name and it will become the 'active' window. If you have lots of items on the 'taskbar' you may not be able to read them all properly, **point** at the name with the mouse and the full title is shown. Or, you can **hold down** the 'Alt' key and **press 'Tab'** to move through all open windows.

Information Technology Resources – User Guide for Windows 95
© ITR 1999

35

*Windows' functions*

## How do I ...?

### Minimize all open windows

If you have lots of open windows, you can minimize them all onto the taskbar with one action. **Hold down** the 'windows' ⊞ key and **press m** or, **point** to a clear area on the taskbar and **right click** or, **click** on a clear area of the taskbar and **press** the 'shortcut' key for the 'shortcut menu'. **Click** on **'Minimize All Windows'** and they all move to the taskbar.

To maximize them all again, **hold down** the 'Shift' key and the 'windows' ⊞ key and **press m** or, **point** to a clear space on the taskbar and **right click** or, **click** on a clear area of the taskbar and **press** the 'shortcut' key for the 'shortcut' menu. **Click** on **'Undo Minimize All'**.

To close a minimized window, **point** to it on the taskbar and **right click** to show this 'shortcut menu'. **Click** on **'Close'**.

*Windows' functions*

# How do I ...?

## Get help

**Press 'F1'** or **click** on the **'Start'** button and **click** on **'Help'** to show this window.  There are 3 different sections - 'Contents', 'Index' and 'Find'.

- 'Contents' groups the help items into topics and this can be very useful when you are first starting to use Windows or even if you have used Windows before.  'Tips and tricks' are worth looking at, as well as 'If you've used Windows before'.
- 'Index' lists all the topics in alphabetical order.  **Key-in** the first few letters of the function to move to that part of the alphabet.  **Double click** on the item you want.  To print out any 'Help' topic **click** on **'Options', 'Print Topic'**.
- 'Find' is the 'Help' database.  **Key-in** the function and 'Windows' searches for anything connected with that item.  If the 'Minimize database size' option is recommended, **choose** it.

In windows with a 'Help' **?** button in the top right corner, **click** on it to attach a question mark to the mouse pointer, **click** on the item you need help with.  Or, **right click** the mouse button on any item and **click** on **'What's This'** to show a help message.

*Windows' functions*

# How do I ...?

## Get out of a program that stops working

You could find that when you are working on your computer, it may 'hang' or 'crash'. This means that it will stop working with something still on the screen. Nothing will happen when you click the mouse and you cannot save your work or leave the 'software' in the way you should. This is one reason why you should save your work often.

**Hold down** the **'Ctrl'** key and the **'Alt'** key and **press 'Delete'**. This window will then show on screen, with the program that has 'hung' highlighted and 'Not responding' alongside it. You can **click** on **'End Task'** and close down the program that has 'hung' but you will lose any unsaved work in that program. You can then continue to work in other programs that are still running. If this does not work **press 'Ctrl'**, **'Alt'** and **'Delete'** again to re-start the computer and lose all unsaved work. Or, you may have to turn off the computer at the power switch. If you do this, 'Scandisk' (see page 85) will run when you start the computer again to check for any faults on the disk.

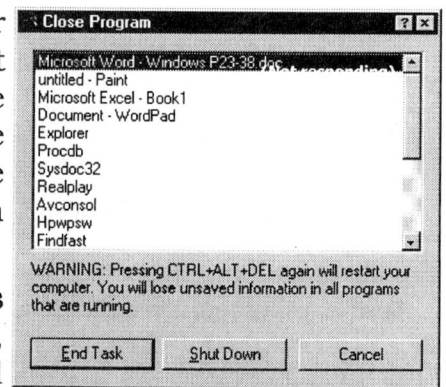

*Windows' functions*

# How do I ...?

## Take the 10 minute tour

This is a very useful feature in 'Help'. It is an 'interactive' demonstration of how to use Windows, which means you must do what it tells you to do before it will move on.  **Press** the 'windows' ⊞ key or **click** on **'Start', 'Help', 'Contents',** and **double click** on **'Tour: Ten minutes to using Windows'** to show this window.  If you cannot run this feature see page 64.

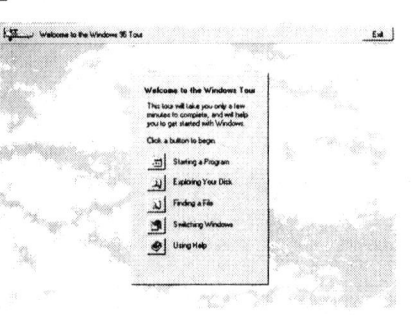

The tour consists of the 5 sections shown.  **Click** on each section and follow the screen instructions.  If you do not understand, **click** on the 'Show Me' button and it will show you what to do.  The flashing vertical line is called the 'cursor' and shows the point where your text will appear.  You must use capital letters where needed or it will not recognise your answer, if you continue to get an answer wrong it will put the correct one in for you.  **Click** on **'Exit Tour'** button to leave or, **click** on **'Exit', 'Exit tour'** at any time to leave without finishing the tour.  You can **click** on the **'Menu'** key inside a section to go back to the list of options.  Work through this several times if you need to.

*Windows' functions*

## How do I ...?

### <u>Organise my files</u>

Files are stored in 'folders'. 'Folders' are holders, they can hold files, other folders or both files and folders. Any 'application software' (see page 15) that you install on your machine will make its own 'folder' as it is written onto the computer and save its program files in it. Any data that you save whilst using an application such as WORD 97 or EXCEL 97 will be saved in the 'My Documents' folder on the hard drive (drive c:). If you just keep saving more and more files into 'My Documents', the time will come when it will be difficult to find files.

Think about the type of files you will be saving. Make new folders (see page 43) inside 'My Documents', give the folders names that mean something and save all files to do with one subject inside its folder. For example, you might put all the letters you write in a folder called 'Letters', or all the work you do for a local club in a folder with the club's name.

Remember you can use long file names with spaces between words, so make the file name meaningful so that you will know what is in it without opening the file.

*Windows' functions*

## How do I ...?

### Look at files and folders with My Computer

To see what is on your computer, you can use 'My Computer'. From the desktop, **double click** on the **'My Computer'** icon in the top left of the screen to open this window. It shows a picture and description of all the disk drives and 'system folders'. Note that if you are connected to a network, the picture of the disk drive will have cables underneath it. **Double click** on the icon for drive (c:). The screen shows all the folders and any files saved on the 'root' of drive c:. The 'root' is the first level of what is called the 'tree' of folders (see page 42).

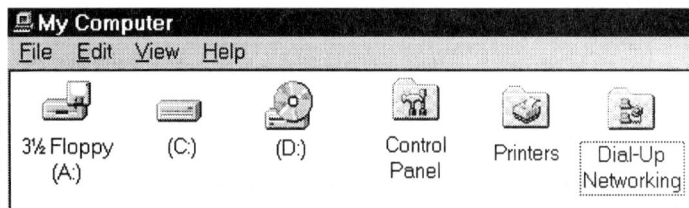

Folders are shown with this picture. Underneath the picture is the name of the folder. You can **double click** on a folder to see what is inside it. You can see which are files because they have a different picture above them. The picture, called the file's 'icon', shows which 'application software' was used to make the file. This icon shows the file was made in WORD 97, the word processing package.

*Windows' functions*

## How do I ...?

### Look at files and folders using Windows Explorer

You can use 'Windows Explorer' to see the files and folders on your computer. **Hold down** the 'windows' key and **press e** or, **click** on **'Start', 'Programs', 'Windows Explorer'** to show this window. Or, you can **click** on the **'My Computer'** icon and **press** the 'shortcut' key or, **right click** while pointing at the **'My Computer'** icon to show the 'shortcut' menu. **Click** on **'Explore'** and **click** on the 'plus' sign (+) next to (c:). Everybody's screen will look different.

The window pane on the left shows all the folders. This diagram of how the folders are stored on the computer is called the 'tree'. The first level of folders is called the 'root', think of this as the trunk of the tree. The next levels are the branches of the 'tree'. When you see a 'plus' sign (+) at the side of a folder, this means there are more folders inside this folder. Each level has more files or folders inside folders and so the 'branches' of the 'tree' are formed. **Click** on the + and – signs and experiment moving through the folders. **Click** on a folder and the icon changes to 🗁 to show it is now open. The contents of the folder are then shown in the pane on the right hand side of the screen.

*Windows' functions*

## How do I ...?

### Make a new folder

You must remember that any new folder you make will be placed inside the folder which you are in at the time, or on the 'root' of the disk drive if that is where you are.  **Open 'Windows Explorer'** (see page 42).  Use the scroll bars (see page 32) to the right of the 'tree' to move up and down through the folders.  **Click** on the **'My Documents'** folder and it turns blue with its contents shown on the right of the screen.

**Click** on **'File'**, **'New'** and **'Folder'**.  A new folder is shown at the bottom of the list on the right of the screen with the words highlighted in blue (see page 52). **Key-in** a name for the folder, there is no need to delete the other words.  If you make a mistake or change your mind after naming a folder, **click** the right mouse button on the name, **click** on **'Rename'** and **key-in** your new name. This folder is now inside the 'My Documents' folder.

Information Technology Resources – User Guide for Windows 95
© ITR 1999

43

*Windows' functions*

## How do I ...?

### Use toolbars

The buttons on the toolbars carry out the same functions as the pull-down menus, but are faster and easier to use. **Point** to each button and wait – the 'tooltip' attached to the mouse pointer is displayed which gives the function of the button. To select an item, **click** on its button. When a button is selected it is lighter in colour. When buttons are 'greyed-out' they are currently not available for you to use.

This toolbar is used in 'Windows Explorer' and 'My Computer'. To show or hide it, **click** on **'View', 'Toolbar'**. When the tick is shown alongside 'Toolbar' it means it is showing.

In the 'Go to a different folder' box, '(C:)' is displayed. The ▼ shows that further options are available. Whenever you see this arrow, click on it to see a list of choices you can make.

You can move toolbars, **point** to the lines at the left of the toolbar, **click** and **drag** to move around the screen. To move it back, **click** on the 'title bar' and **drag** to the top of the screen. To move the taskbar, **click** on a clear space on it and **drag** it to the top, left or right of the screen.

44  Information Technology Resources – User Guide for Windows 95
© ITR 1999

*Windows' functions*

# How do I ...?

## **Move from one folder to another**

If you are using 'Windows Explorer' to see the 'tree' of files and folders (see page 42) on your computer, you can **click** on a folder in the left 'pane' to open it and see its contents shown on the right of the screen.

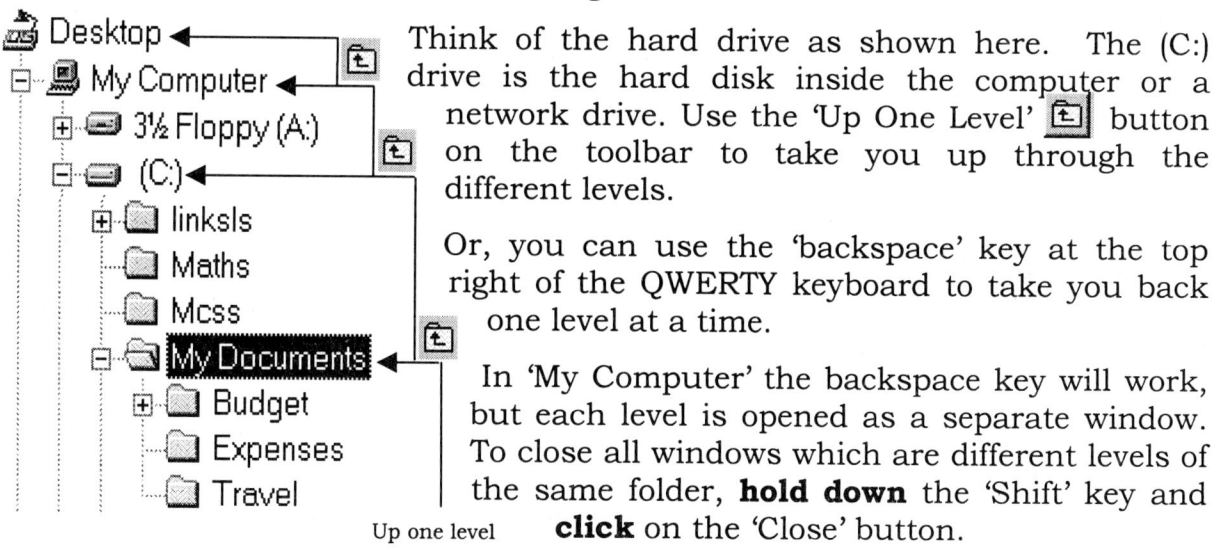

```
Desktop
└─ My Computer
   ├─ 3½ Floppy (A:)
   └─ (C:)
      ├─ linksls
      ├─ Maths
      ├─ Mcss
      └─ My Documents
         ├─ Budget
         ├─ Expenses
         └─ Travel
```
Up one level

Think of the hard drive as shown here. The (C:) drive is the hard disk inside the computer or a network drive. Use the 'Up One Level' button on the toolbar to take you up through the different levels.

Or, you can use the 'backspace' key at the top right of the QWERTY keyboard to take you back one level at a time.

In 'My Computer' the backspace key will work, but each level is opened as a separate window. To close all windows which are different levels of the same folder, **hold down** the 'Shift' key and **click** on the 'Close' button.

Information Technology Resources – User Guide for Windows 95
© ITR 1999

45

*Windows' functions*

## How do I ...?

### Change the way my files and folders are shown

**Open 'Windows Explorer'** or **'My Computer'** (see pages 42 and 41). **Click** on the **'View'** menu to show these choices. Any item with a tick is turned on. **Click** on **'Toolbar'** and **'Status Bar'** to turn them off and again to turn them on. These are called 'toggle' switches. Notice that when you point to a menu item, the 'status bar' shows what will happen if you 'select' it. **Click** on a folder in the left 'pane' and the 'status bar' shows the number of 'objects', these can be files or folders, it holds. It also shows the total size of all the 'objects' in the folder.

You can view the files and folders in other ways. **Click** on these buttons on the 'toolbar' (see page 44) or **click** on **'Large Icons'**, **'Small Icons'**, **'List'** or **'Details'** on the menu. In 'Details', 'Modified' shows the date and time the file was first made or last changed. **Click** on **'Arrange Icons'** to see a further menu to show files in name, type, size or date order. If you had changed the floppy disk in drive A:, **'Refresh'** would list the contents of the new disk to update the screen display. Or, you can **press F5** to refresh the screen. For **'Options'** see pages 47 and 48.

46         Information Technology Resources – User Guide for Windows 95
                              © ITR 1999

*Windows' functions*

# How do I ...?

### Show file extensions and hidden files

Windows saves files as the name, a dot and a 3-letter 'file extension', which will not automatically show on your screen. The extension shows the program used to make the file; WORD 97 uses **'.doc'**, EXCEL 97 **'.xls'** and WINZIP **'.zip'**. WINZIP saves files in a special way to take up less space on the disk. To see all extensions, **open 'Windows Explorer'** (see page 42) and **click** on **'View', 'Options'** and **'View'** tab to show this window. **Click** on **'Hide MS-DOS file extensions for file types that are registered'** to remove the tick.

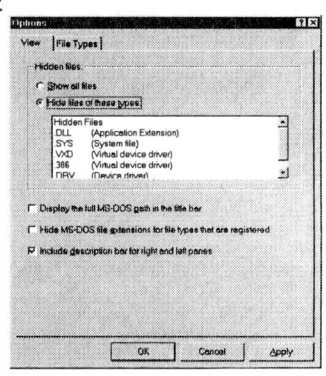

Some files used to run the computer are hidden so that you cannot delete or change them by mistake. To see all the files, **click** on **'Show all files'**. **Click** on **'Display the full MS-DOS path in the title bar'**, to see at the top of the screen the disk drive you are working on and the folder or folders you have opened to find the file or folder you are in. To see descriptions above the 2 window panes in the 'Windows Explorer' screen, make sure there is a tick alongside **'Include description bars for right and left panes'**. **Click** on the 'help' **?** button (see page 37) for more information. **Click** on **'OK'**.

Information Technology Resources – User Guide for Windows 95
© ITR 1999

47

***Windows' functions***

# How do I ...?

## Find out what a file's icon means

**Open 'Windows Explorer'**, **click** on **'View'**, **'Options'**, and **'File Types'** tab to see this window. In the 'Registered file types' box is a list of the types of files on your computer with their icons at the side of them.

**Click** on a file and the 'File type details' box shows the icon and the extension which is given to the file name, as well as showing the file which will open the application software it was created in. These files are called 'exe' files, because their file extension is **'.exe'**. These are files which 'execute' a program, that is they make something happen on the computer rather than just holding information. In the example above, the file extension is '.doc' and the file could be opened using 'Winword.exe', this is the name of the file which loads Microsoft WORD 97.

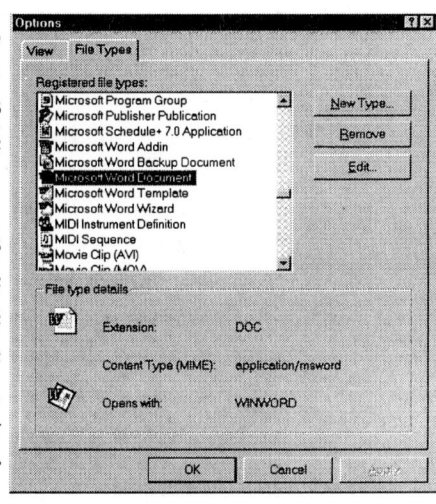

You can add new types, and remove or edit ones already on your list.

*Windows' functions*

# How do I ...?

## Format a floppy disk

Most disks are formatted when you buy them, which means they have had markings put onto them so that the computer can store and find data. You may want to format a disk to remove files or damaged areas. **Open 'My Computer'** or **'Windows Explorer'**. **Point** at the icon for 'Floppy A:' and **right click** for the 'shortcut menu'. **Click** on **'Format'** to show this window. **Check** the 'title bar' shows 'Floppy A:', as formatting can delete the contents of the disk. The capacity, that is the size, must match the disk you are using. **Click** on **'Quick'** to erase the contents of your disk. **Click 'Full'** for new disks or those which may be damaged. **Click** on **'Copy system files only'** to make a disk to start your computer, but without losing data already stored on the disk.

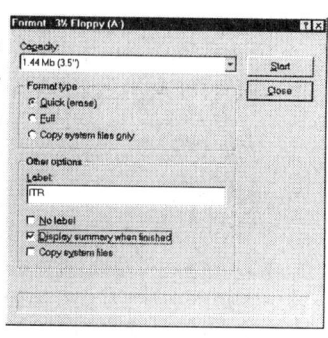

**Click** under **'Label'** and **key-in** a name for your disk of up to 11 letters or numbers. Leave the tick by **'Display summary when finished'** and it will show whether any 'bad sectors', faults on the disk, were found. **Click 'Copy system files'** to add the system files to a new disk after formatting. **Click** on **'Start'** and follow the screen prompts.

*Windows' functions*

# How do I ...?

## Make a copy of a floppy disk

Put the disk to be copied into 'Drive A:'. **Open 'My Computer'**, or **'Windows Explorer', point** at **'Floppy A:'** and **right click** the mouse button. **Click** on **'Copy Disk'** from the 'shortcut menu' to show this window. You are going to copy from one floppy disk to another floppy disk.

**Click** on **'Start'**, and a message at the bottom of the window shows the computer is reading the files on the 'source disk', the one you are copying from. These are being copied into the RAM memory (see page 14). A message tells you to insert the 'destination disk', the one you are copying to, and **click** on **'OK'**. The files are then copied from the RAM memory onto the second disk. The window shows the computer is writing to the 'destination disk'. When the copying is finished, a message will tell you if it has been successful.

*Windows' functions*

# How do I ...?

## Select files or folders

'Housekeeping' is an important function.  Regularly check that you have made 'backup' copies (see page 86) of important files, have emptied your 'Recycle Bin' (see page 30) and have removed (deleted) unwanted files, including temporary files (see page 53), internet history files (see page 81) and folders.  If you do not do this, then your machine will work more slowly than it should.  **Open 'My Computer'** to see the files on your disks.  To show the files as a list **click** on **'View', 'List'**.  Or, **open 'Windows Explorer'** (see page 42).  When you have the list of files on your screen, make sure that the screen is 'maximized' (see page 26) so you can see as many files as possible.

To select a file or folder, **click** on its name.  To select a group of files next to each other, **click** on the first one, **hold down** the 'Shift' key and **click** on the last one.  Everything between the 2 clicks is highlighted.  Or, you can **point** at the end of the last file name, **hold down** the left mouse button and **drag** up over the files.  As you drag a box appears on screen and all the files inside the box are highlighted.  Or, you can **click** anywhere on a list of files, **hold down** the 'Ctrl' key and **press a** to select all the files in the list.  To select files which are not next to each other, **hold down** the 'Ctrl' key and **click** on each file.

*Windows' functions*

## How do I ...?

### Delete, print, open and rename files

**Open 'Windows Explorer'** or **'My Computer'**, **select** the files or folders (see page 51) to be removed and **press 'Delete'** key or **click** on the 'Delete' ❌ button. If you **hold down** the 'Shift' key and **press 'Delete'** the file does not go to the 'Recycle Bin'. Or, **point** at the file or folder, **right click** for the 'shortcut menu' (yours may look different) and **click** on **'Delete'**. Deleting a folder removes all the files and folders inside it (see page 42). **Click** on the 'Undo' ↶ button, **'Ctrl z'** or **'Edit', 'Undo'** to undo. Use this 'shortcut menu' to open or print selected files. **Double click** on a file to open it and its software.

To rename a file or folder, **click** on it and **press 'F2'** or 'shortcut' key or **point** to it and **right click** for the 'shortcut menu', **click** on **'Rename'**. A box appears round the name, which changes colour, and a cursor is flashing at the end. Do not delete, just **key-in** your new name and the old one is replaced. You must not change the file extension (see page 47) or the file may become unusable. To go back to the original name, **point** away from the file name on the same side of the window and **right click**, then **click** on **'Undo Rename'** or **click** on the 'Undo' button.

52

Information Technology Resources – User Guide for Windows 95
© ITR 1999

*Windows' functions*

## How do I ...?

### Delete temporary files

Most 'application software' creates backup files, which means your work will be saved on a regular basis. If you have a power failure or some other problem, you can go to the backup file and **double click** on it to open it. However, the 'system software' makes notes for itself in the form of temporary files which are of no use and should be removed on a regular basis to free disk space.

**Open 'Windows Explorer'** and **click** on **'Windows', 'Temp'** to see these backup files and the temporary files which have the 'file extension' **'.tmp'**. The number of files is shown on the 'status bar' in the bottom left corner of the screen. As some files may be in use, it is better to view them in date order. **Click** on **'View', 'Arrange Icons', 'by Date'**. The most recent files are then shown at the top. Leave the ones with today's date and **click** on the first one beneath them, scroll down to the bottom of the list, **hold down** the 'Shift' key and **click** on the last one in the list. All the files between the 2 clicks are highlighted. **Hold down** the 'Shift' key and **press 'Delete'** and the files are removed without going to the 'Recycle Bin'. If you do include any files that are in use, Windows will tell you they cannot be deleted. If you use the internet, you should remove the contents of 'Temporary Internet Files' (see also page 81).

*Windows' functions*

## How do I ...?

### Copy files and folders

**Open 'My Computer'** or **'Windows Explorer'**.  To copy a single file, **point** to the file name and **right click** for this 'shortcut menu'.  Note that when a folder is selected, another option 'Explore' appears at the top of the menu.  For more than one file or folder, **select** them first and **press** the 'shortcut' key to open the 'shortcut menu' and **click** on **'Copy'**.  Or, you can **click** on **'Send To'** to copy a file directly to the floppy disk or 'My Briefcase' (see page 56).  **Click** on the file's new position, **open** the 'shortcut menu' and **click** on **'Paste'**, which will now be included on the menu.

Or, you can select the files and **click** on the 'Copy' button or **'Ctrl C'**, or **click** on **'Edit', 'Copy'**.  A copy of the files or folders is made in the computer's temporary memory (RAM) (see page 14), though nothing happens on screen.  **Click** on the file's new place and **click** on the 'Paste' button or **press 'Ctrl V'**, or **click** on **'Edit', 'Paste'**.  Or, you can use 'drag and drop' for copying (see page 55).  **Select** the files or folders to copy **point** anywhere in the highlighting and **click** and **hold down** the right mouse button.  **Drag** until the new position is selected, that is it changes colour, and **click** on **'Copy Here'**.

*Windows' functions*

# How do I ...?

## <u>Move files and folders</u>

**Open 'My Computer'** or **'Windows Explorer'**. Point at the file or folder to move, **right click** for the 'shortcut menu' and **click** on **'Cut'**. Or, **select** the files or folders and **click** on the 'Cut' ✂ button or **press 'Ctrl X'** or **click** on **'Edit'**, **'Cut'**. The file or folder's icon is 'greyed-out' on screen. **Click** on the new place for your file or folder and **click** on **'Paste'** from the 'shortcut menu' or **click** on the 'Paste' 📋 button or **press 'Ctrl V'** or **click** on **'Edit'**, **'Paste'**. To move several files or folders, **select** them first (see page 51) and use one of these methods.

Or, you can use 'drag and drop' to move. **Point** at the file or folder, or anywhere inside the blue highlighting for more than one file or folder, **hold down** the right mouse button and **drag** to the new position. **Click** on **'Move Here'**. **Click** on **'Edit'**, **'Undo Move'** to put the files or folders back.

You can also use the left mouse button for 'drag and drop' copying or moving. To move files on the same disk drive **click** on the files and **drag** to the new position. To move files onto a different disk drive **hold down** the 'Shift' key while you **drag.** To copy files on the same drive **hold down** the 'Ctrl' key while you **drag**. To copy files onto a different disk drive **drag** and **drop**.

*Windows' functions*

## How do I ...?

### Use My Briefcase to update files on separate computers

'My Briefcase' lets you copy files from one computer onto a floppy disk, take the disk to another computer, a laptop or a machine at home, make changes to the files and automatically update the original files saved on the first computer. This function also works between 2 computers joined together in a network or by cables. **Open 'Windows Explorer'** and **click** on the **'Restore'** button (see page 26) so that you can see that window and the desktop. **Click** on the files to be copied (see page 51). **Drag** these files to the **'My Briefcase'** icon on the desktop, this will make a copy of your files into 'My Briefcase'. **Drag** the **'My Briefcase'** icon from the desktop onto the '3½ Floppy (A:)' disk drive in the left pane of 'Windows Explorer'. This moves the 'My Briefcase' icon to 'Floppy A:'.

**Remove** the floppy disk and insert it in the second computer. **Open 'Windows Explorer'** and **double click** on the files to be changed to open them. Make your changes and save in the usual way. Return the floppy disk to the first computer and **open 'Windows Explorer'**. **Drag** the 'My Briefcase' icon from '3½ Floppy (A:)' onto the desktop. **Double click** on the icon to open 'My Briefcase'. **Click** on **'Briefcase'**, **'Update all'** and **'Update'** to change the original file to the new version, or **select** files and **click** on **'Update Selection'**.

*Windows' functions*

## How do I ...?

### Find files or folders

**Hold down** the 'windows' ⊞ key and **press 'f'** or **click** on **'Start'**, **'Find'**, **'Files or Folders'** to show this window. In the 'Named' box **key-in** all or part of the file name. **Click** on **'Browse'** to choose a drive to be searched other than the C: drive. **Click** on **'Include subfolders'** to remove the tick and ignore this option.

**Click** on the **'Date Modified'** tab if you want to find files or folders which were changed on a certain date or within a period of time which you can set yourself. **Click** on the **'Advanced'** tab and **click** on ▼ alongside the 'Of type:' box to see a list of file types (see page 47) **click** on one of these or leave it at 'All Files and Folders' for a full search. You can also ask Windows to find files which contain certain text or are of a certain size. If you want the text to be searched for to match exactly what you have keyed-in, **click** on **'Options'**, **'Case Sensitive'**. To help limit the search, use words which are unique to that file. **Point** to any item, **click** the right mouse button and **click** with the left mouse button on **'What's This?'** for an explanation of that item. **Click** on **'Find now'** to start the search (see page 58).

Information Technology Resources – User Guide for Windows 95
© ITR 1999

57

*Windows' functions*

# How do I ...?

## Save the results of a search

When Windows has completed your search it will give the results in this 'dialogue box'. You can **double click** on a file's icon to open it. If you cannot read the full address of the file, **point** to the vertical line between 'In Folder' and 'Size'. The mouse pointer becomes a ◄║►. **Click** and **drag** the line to the right to see the contents of the column.

**Click** on **'Options'**, **'Save Results'** if you want to save the results of the search with the search details. If you want to save just the details and not the results, **click** on **'Options'** and make sure there is not a tick beside 'Save Results', if there is, **click** to remove it. Whichever you choose, **click** on **'File'**, **'Save Search'**. An icon for the search is put onto your desktop.

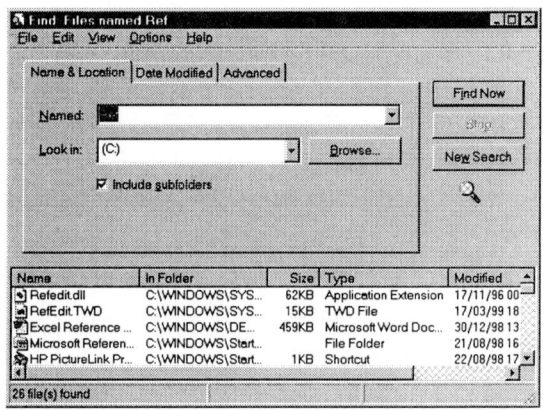

**Double click** on the icon on the desktop and **click** on **'Find Now'** to run the search again if you did not save the results.

58     Information Technology Resources – User Guide for Windows 95
© ITR 1999

*Windows' functions*

## How do I ...?

### Find the most recently-used files

**Press** the 'windows' ⊞ key or **click** on **'Start', point** at **'Documents'** and a second menu is shown. This contains a list of the last 15 documents that you used. **Double click** on the file you want, to open the 'application software' it was made in and the file itself.

This is a useful way of quickly opening files which you have used in your last session.

You can delete the contents of this list (see page 100).

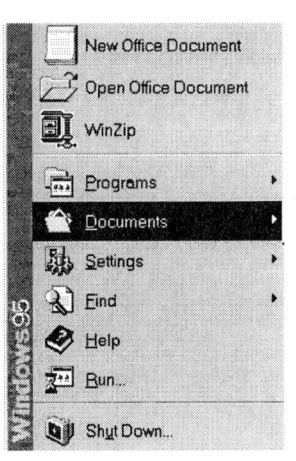

*Windows' functions*

## How do I ...?

### Use the Control Panel

Control Panel is used for changing the settings on your computer. **Press** the 'windows' ⊞ key or, **click** on **'Start', 'Settings', 'Control Panel'** to show this window. You can change many of the settings for Windows here. The ones you will probably use the most will have a separate page showing you how to use them. Others you may not need to use, such as 'Find Fast'. This builds indexes which help to speed up finding documents from the 'Open' 'dialogue box' in your Microsoft Office applications. **Double click** on **'Find Fast', 'Index', 'Show Indexer Log'** to see the starting times of your computer sessions.

When a window gives the choices **'OK'** and **'Apply', choose 'OK'** to save and leave the window and **'Apply'** to save the setting but keep the window open.

*Windows' functions*

# How do I ...?

## Choose Accessibility options

**Press** the 'windows' ⊞ key or, **click** on **'Start'**, **'Settings'**, **'Control Panel'** and **double click** on **'Accessibility Options'** to show this window. If you have trouble using the keyboard, you can get help with 'StickyKeys', 'FilterKeys' and 'ToggleKeys'. An explanation of each is given on this page, **click** on your choice and **click** on **'Apply'**.

On the 'Sound' tab you can set the computer to show on screen what you would normally hear. The 'Display' tab lets you set colours which are easier to read if your eyesight is not good. In 'General' you can choose to turn these functions off if the machine has been idle for so many minutes or, to give a sound or message on screen when the features are turned off. Or, for people who cannot use the keyboard and mouse, you can choose to add a different 'input device' to your computer, this is another way of entering data. **Look** in the 'Settings' box to see the 'shortcut' for these functions, you can then turn them on and off at the keyboard. Useful for different users of the same machine. **Click** on **'OK'**.

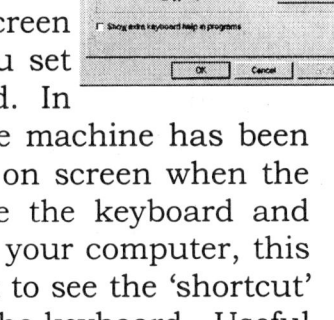

*Windows' functions*

## How do I ...?

### Add new hardware

If you buy a new printer or modem, or any piece of 'hardware' you just plug it in and switch on your computer. Windows will find the new hardware, this is called 'Plug and Play', and take you through this 'Add New Hardware Wizard'. A 'wizard' takes you step-by-step through the options available to complete a task. Or, **press** the 'windows' ⊞ key or **click** on **'Start'**, **'Settings'**, **'Control Panel'** and **double click** on **'Add New Hardware'** to run the wizard yourself.

Your new hardware should come with a disk or CD ROM with its own 'drivers', these allow you to run the hardware using the best settings. If not, you may find some on your Windows CD ROM. If you have a disk or CD ROM, **click** on **'Have Disk'** when you see this option. If you do not have a disk, Windows will find the nearest alternative for you, or, if you have a modem, you can download drivers from the Microsoft Windows' Driver Library on the Internet at **http://www.microsoft.com**.

*Windows' functions*

## How do I ...?

### Add or remove programs

If you want to 'install', that means add, a new software application onto your computer, you can do this through 'Control Panel' and it is then easier to 'uninstall' it later. However, many programs will install themselves from their own CD ROM.

**Press** the 'windows' ⊞ key or, **click** on **'Start'**, **'Settings'**, **'Control Panel'** and **double click** on **'Add/Remove Programs'** to show this window. You will see a list of all the programs on your computer; everyone's will look different. **Click** on **'Install'** to add a new program and follow the screen messages. Or, **click** on one of the listed programs and **click** on **'Add/Remove'** to either remove a program or 're-install' a program already on the machine with different settings.

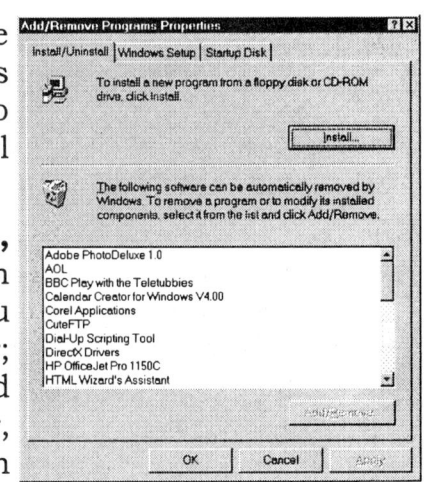

**Click** on the 'Windows Setup' tab for adding or removing items from your Windows setup (see page 64). In 'Startup Disk' you can make a disk to start your machine in an emergency. It is a good idea to make one of these.

*Windows' functions*

# How do I ...?

## Add new items to installed software

When Windows is installed, a 'Typical' installation is usually chosen. This means that not every part of every 'component', that is a section of the software, is copied. This keeps the size of the program much smaller, and users can then add other 'components' as and when they need them.

**Press** the 'windows' ⊞ key or, **click** on **'Start'**, **'Settings'**, **'Control Panel'** and **double click** on **'Add/Remove Programs'** and **'Windows Setup'** tab to show this window. In the 'Components' box is a list of all the extras you can add to your Windows program. **Click** on a name and **click** on **'Details'** to see the items this 'component' includes. Each item shows its size, **click** on an item to put a tick alongside it. **Click** to remove ticks on any items you do not want. Think carefully about the space you have available on your machine before choosing too many items. **Click** on **'OK'** to install the new items. You may be asked for the Windows CD ROM or installation disk. This is the way you can add items such as the 'Tour: Ten minutes to using Windows' (see page 39), the 'Backup' feature (see page 86) and 'Multimedia sound schemes' (see page 79).

*Windows' functions*

# How do I ...?

## Set the date and time

**Double click** on the 24-hour clock in the 'notification area' of the taskbar or, **press** the 'windows' ⊞ key or **click** on **'Start'**, **'Settings'**, **'Control Panel'**, and **double click** on **'Date/Time'** to show this 'window'. The calendar shows the current date. To change it, **click** on ▼ next to the month and **click** on the correct one. You can do the same for the year. As you change the month, the blue square around the date moves to the new setting.

The clock shows the time in 12 and 24-hour format. To change the clock, **drag** over any wrong numbers in the 24-hour box and **key-in** your correction. Note the 12-hour clock changes as you key-in the different numbers. **Click** on 'Time Zone' and choose the area of the world you are working in, for the United Kingdom it is **'(GMT) Greenwich Mean Time: Dublin, Edinburgh, London, Lisbon'**. If 'Automatically adjust clock for daylight saving changes' does not have a tick alongside it, **click** on it. The computer will then update its clock when we change our clocks in spring and autumn. The new settings will then be shown on the 'Date & Time' tab. **Click** on **'OK'**. See also page 78.

*Windows' functions*

## How do I ...?
### Change the background of my desktop

**Point** at a blank area of the desktop and **click** the right mouse button for the 'shortcut menu' and **click** on the 'Properties' tab, or **press** the 'windows' ⊞ key or, **click** on 'Start', 'Settings', 'Control Panel' and **double click** on 'Display' to show this 'window'. You can use a pattern for your desktop from the list or, you can choose one then edit it and save your changes by using 'Edit pattern'.

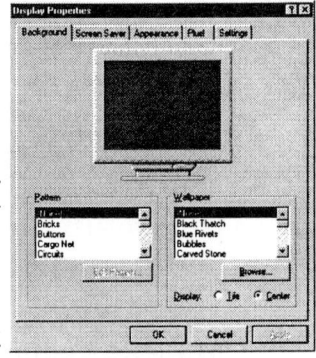

You can **click** on a 'Wallpaper' from the list or **click** on 'Browse' and find a file of your own to use which is then added to the list of wallpapers available. This file could be a drawing or scanned photograph saved as a 'bitmap', that means it was made using software which could save it with the 'file extension' '.bmp' (see page 47). If you use the 'Paint' program (see page 91) **click** on 'File', Set as Wallpaper (Tiled) or 'Set as Wallpaper (Centered)' to also add the bitmap to your list of wallpapers. **Click** on 'Tile' for the wallpaper to cover the whole screen or, **click** on 'Centre' for a picture in the middle of the screen (see page 68). You can use both patterns and wallpapers together, but if you choose 'Tile' you will not see the pattern. **Click** on 'OK'.

Information Technology Resources – User Guide for Windows 95
© ITR 1999

66

*Windows' functions*

## How do I ...?

### Change my screen saver and appearance of windows on screen

**Open** the **'Display Properties'** window (see page 66) and **click** on the **'Screen Saver'** tab to show this window. The 'screen saver' appears when your keyboard is not used for the number of minutes shown under **'Wait'** and saves wear and tear on the monitor. **Click** on your choice under **'Screen Saver'**. **Click** on **'Preview'** to see it work on the full screen and **click** again to go back to this window. If you choose **'3-D Text'** as a screen saver, you can **click** on **'Settings'** and input a message. **Click** on **'Password protected'** if you want to set a password to remove the screen saver – useful when working on confidential documents.

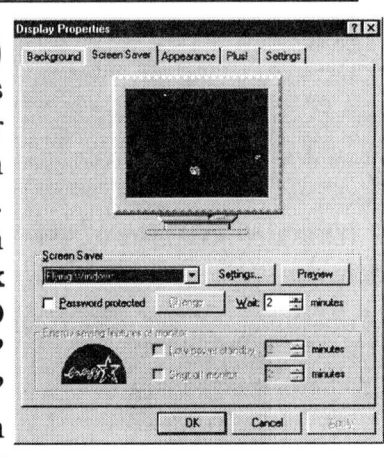

**Click** on the **'Appearance'** tab and **click** on ▼ under **'Scheme'** to show a list of colour schemes you can choose for your screen. Or, you can **click** on ▼ under **'Item'** and choose different parts of the scheme to change such as the colour of your desktop and then **click** on **'OK'** or **'Save As'** and name this new scheme. This scheme name is then included in the list.

*Windows' functions*

# How do I ...?

## Change the icons on my desktop and colour settings

**Open** the **'Display Properties'** window (see page 66) and **click** on the **'Plus!'** tab to show this window. To change the icons on your desktop, **click** on the one to be changed, **click** on **'Change Icon'** and choose another from those given. **Click** on **'Default Icon'** to change back to the usual setting.

Try experimenting with the other options given in this window. **Click** on **'Stretch desktop wallpaper to fit the screen'** to change a centred wallpaper to the full size of the screen.

**Click** on the **'Settings'** tab to change the **'Colour Palette'**. Some programs need certain colour settings before they can work. This is where you can make that change. You can also change the size of the 'font', that is the writing, in Windows, or, you can change the desktop area to show less or more information. **Click** on **'Apply'** to save the settings and stay on that page or **'OK'** to save the settings and close **'Display Properties'**.

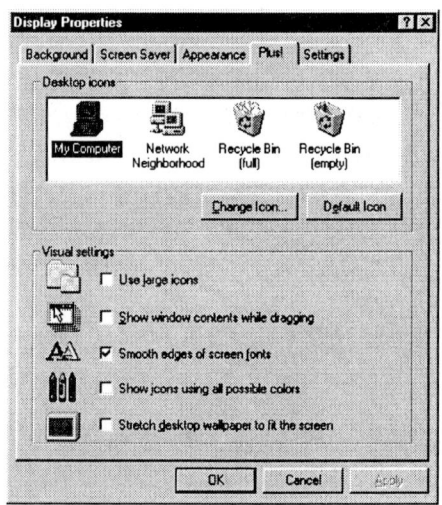

*Windows' functions*

## How do I ...?

### See the fonts stored on my computer

**Press** the 'windows' ⊞ key or, **click** on 'Start', 'Settings', Control Panel' and **double click** on 'Fonts' to show this window. This is a list of the fonts, these are the different styles of writing, that are saved on your computer. Everyone's will look different. You use this window to remove or add, 'install', new fonts onto your machine. The 2 T's show it is a 'True Type' font, which means that what you see on screen is how it will print out.

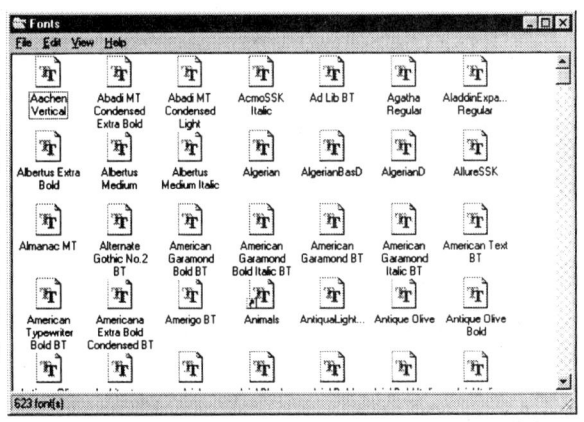

**Click** on 'File', 'Install New Font' and follow the instructions on screen to add a new font. Check that the **'Copy fonts to Fonts folder'** box is ticked. **Click** on a font to 'select' it and **click** on 'File', 'Delete' to remove it. **Double click** on any font and a page appears on screen which shows you how that font will print, you can then **click** on 'Print' to print out a copy or 'Done' to go back to this window.

*Windows' functions*

## How do I ...?

### Change the internet settings

**Right click** on 'The Internet' icon at the desktop for the 'shortcut menu' and **click** on **'Properties'** or **press** the 'windows' ⊞ key or, **click** on **'Start'**, **'Settings'**, **'Control Panel'** and **double click** on **'Internet'** to show this window. Under **'Multimedia'** you can choose to turn off pictures, sounds and video clips to load your web pages more quickly. You can use Windows' colours or choose your own. Or, you can choose the colour of the links on the web page. They are usually underlined and blue before you click on them and purple afterwards. You can also select items for your web page toolbar and the font that will be used.

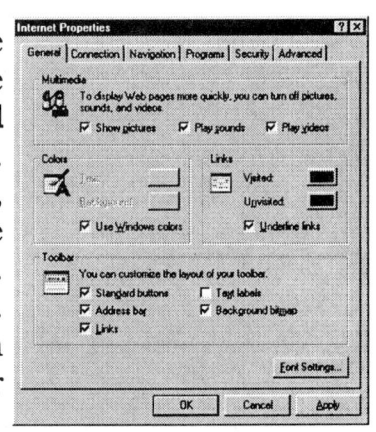

**Click** on the other page tabs to see features of the internet which you can change. In the **'Security'** tab you can set the things that other users, probably children, can view on the internet. **Click** on **'Settings'** to use a password (see page 75) so that others cannot make changes. If you use the internet often, reduce the number of days that pages are kept in the 'History' folder in the **'Navigation'** tab (see also page 53). **Click** on **'OK'** to save your new settings.

*Windows' functions*

## How do I ...?

### Change the settings for my keyboard

If you are having trouble with the keyboard, you can change its settings at this window. **Press** the 'windows' ⊞ key or, **click** on **'Start'**, **'Settings'**, **'Control Panel'** and **double click** on **'Keyboard'**. If you find that keys repeat because you hold them down too long, **click** and **drag** the slider under 'Repeat delay' towards **'Long'**. You can also change the speed that letters are repeated, **drag** the slider under 'Repeat rate' towards **'Slow'**. You can test out your new settings in the box below these sliders and adjust them to suit yourself.

You can change the speed that the cursor, the flashing line which shows where the text you key-in will appear, blinks. Experiment and see how the cursor under 'Cursor blink rate' changes.

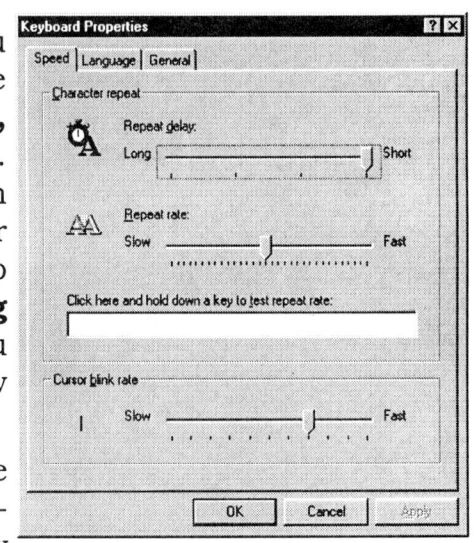

Other settings in this window, include changing the language that you want the keyboard to use and the type of keyboard itself.

*Windows' functions*

## How do I ...?

### Set up my machine to send a fax

**'Fax'** means 'facsimile transmission' where data is sent down the telephone lines to another fax machine and is printed out as soon as it is sent or it can be sent to another computer. **Press** the 'windows' ⊞ key or, **click** on **'Start'**, **'Settings'**, **'Control Panel'** and **double click** on **'Mail and Fax'** to show this window. With **'Microsoft Fax'** highlighted, **click** on **'Properties'**. The next window has 4 tabs, **'Message'**, **'Dialling'**, **'Modem'** and **'User'**. In the **'Message'** window are the settings for sending faxes as well as the cover pages you can send. In the **'Dialling'** tab **click** on **'Dialling Properties'** to set a number you might use to get an outside line before dialling a telephone number. In **'Modem'** you can check your modem settings.

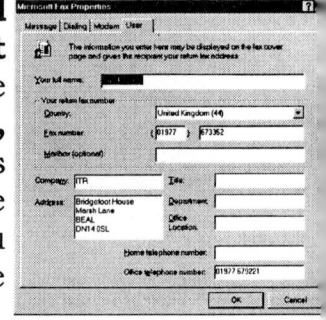

**Click** on the **'User'** tab to show this second window. Here you can enter details which will be used on your fax cover page as well as the telephone number which is your 'default location', that is the number from which you will always dial a fax number unless you change it.

*Windows' functions*

# How do I ...?

## See the settings for my modem

**Press** the 'windows' ⊞ key or, **click** on **'Start'**, **'Settings'**, **'Control Panel'**, and **double click** on **'Modems'** to show this window. It will give you details about the modem you have set up on your computer. In this case the modem is 'external' that is it is outside the computer. You can add or remove modems at this window.

**Click** on **'Properties'** to see which 'port', point of connection, the modem is attached to. This one is using COM2, Communications Port 2. You can also change the speaker volume and choose the speed at which it will work. Your manual for the modem should tell you this.

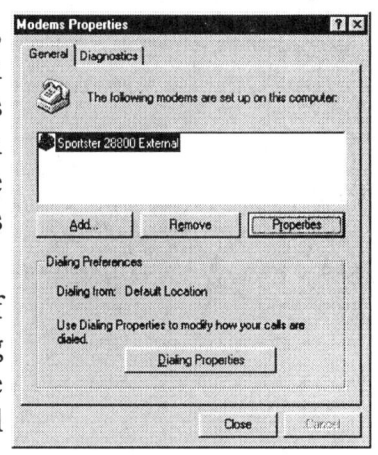

**Click** on **'OK'** and **click** on the **'Diagnostics'** tab to see a list of the ports and what is attached to them, you will see the mouse is using 'COM1'. **Click** on the **'General'** tab and **click** on **'Dialling Properties'**. This shows the location and area code you are using and lets you put in a number which you might have to dial to get an outside line. You can also choose 'tone' or 'pulse' dialling.

*Windows' functions*

# How do I ...?

## Change the style of my mouse pointer

**Press** the 'windows' ⊞ key or, **click** on **'Start'**, **'Settings'**, **'Control Panel, double click** on **'Mouse'** and **click** on the **'Pointers'** tab to see this window. **Click** on ▼ under 'Schemes' and see the choices available. Or, you can **click** on a mouse pointer in the list, **click** on **'Browse'** to see other pointers you can choose and **click** on one to change the way your pointer will look. **Click** on **'Use Default'** to change back to the usual setting.

If you are using a laptop, that is a portable computer, it is a good idea to put trails on the mouse pointer. This makes it easier to see it on the small screen. **Click** on the **'Motion'** tab to see the options available.

**Click** on the **'General'** tab to change the type of mouse you are using.

*Windows' functions*

# How do I ...?

## Allow different users to have their own Windows' settings

If more than one person uses a computer, you may want to each have your own Windows' settings. This can be done through 'Password Properties'. **Press** the 'windows' ⊞ key or, **click** on **'Start'**, **'Settings'**, **'Control Panel'** and **double click** on **'Passwords'** to show this window.

The setting shows that all users use the same settings. **Click** on **'Users can customize ...'** and **'User Profile Settings'** then shows that you can have your own desktop icons and other settings. You will have to restart your computer for this setting to take effect.

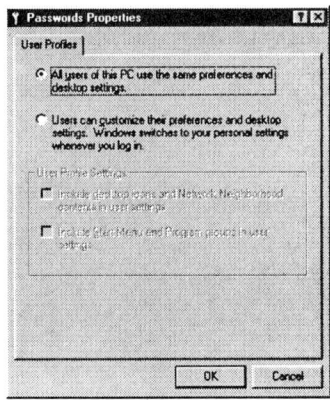

When you start the computer you will be asked for a 'User Name' and 'Password'. **Key-in** your name and a password of letters, numbers or both, you will have to confirm the password. When you **key-in** a password, it shows on screen as stars (*****) so that no-one else can read and use it. Each user can have their own favourite settings and desktop. **Click** on **'Passwords'** and **click** on the first option to take the passwords off. Always keep copies of any passwords that you choose in a safe place.

Information Technology Resources – User Guide for Windows 95
© ITR 1999

75

*Windows' functions*

## How do I ...?

### Add a printer to my computer

If you buy a new printer and plug it into the computer before you switch on the computer, 'Plug and Play' (see page 62) will install it for you. However, you can add a printer yourself. **Press** the 'windows' ⊞ key or **click** on **'Start'**, **'Settings'**, **'Printers'** or **double click** on **'Printers'** in the 'Control Panel' to show this window. Yours will look different.

**Double click** on **'Add Printer'** to start the 'Add Printer Wizard'. You will be shown a list of printer makes and you can choose your printer from this list, but it is better to use a disk or CD ROM which came with the printer. In that case, **click** on **'Have Disk'**. Follow the screen messages to complete the Wizard.

If you want to make a printer the 'default' Windows printer, that is the one it will always choose, **click** on the printer's 'icon' and **click** on **'File'**, **'Set as Default'**. You can still choose any other printer from the 'Print dialogue box' when printing 'Help' topics, or from Notepad or WordPad.

*Windows' functions*

# How do I ...?

## Stop a document printing

When you send a document to print, a printer icon appears on the 'notification area' of the 'taskbar' (see page 20).  **Double click** on this icon to see the printer window which will show you the document name, its 'status' whether it is printing or waiting in a queue, the 'owner', who sent it to print, the 'progress' and what time the print job was started.

To stop the printing, **point** to the document name and **right click** and **click** on **'Cancel Printing'** to remove the print job, or **'Pause Printing'** to stop it until you start it again. To do this, **click** on **'Pause Printing'** again. However, this icon disappears from the 'notification area' when all the data has been sent to the printer, so for a small print job, it may disappear before you can open it.

You can use the Printers folder for deleting print jobs. **Press** the 'windows' key or, **click** on **'Start', 'Settings', 'Printers'** and **double click** on the 'icon' for the printer you are using. **Point** to the document you want removing from the print queue and **right click** for the 'shortcut' menu as above. Once all the document has been sent from the computer to the printer, you will have to use the buttons on your printer to stop the printing process.

*Windows' functions*

## How do I ...?

## Change the Regional Settings on my computer

'Regional Settings' change the way that the computer will show numbers, currency, time and date. **Press** the 'windows' ⊞ key or **click** on **'Start', 'Settings', 'Control Panel'** and **double click** on **'Regional Settings'** to show this window.   Above the map it shows the language you will be using, **'English'** and the version is **'British'**. **Click** to drop down the list of options available if this is not correct.

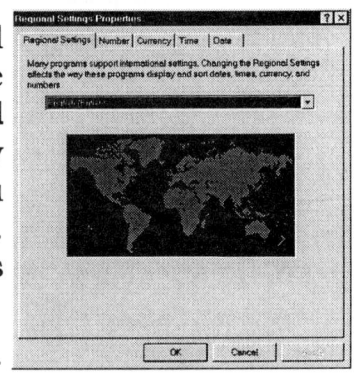

**Click** on each of the tabs to see the settings for each one. In the **'Number'** tab it shows the symbol used for the decimal place, how many numbers come after the decimal place and how negative numbers will be shown.  The **'Currency'** tab shows that the £ sign will be used for money, this would change for other countries.  In the **'Time'** tab you can choose to include **'am'** and **'pm'** rather than the 24-hour clock.  In the **'Date'** tab you can see how the 'short' and 'long' dates will be shown.  In the 'Short date style' **click** on the option for **'d/M/yy'** and 'Long date style' **choose 'd MMMM yyyy'** to avoid a zero (0) at the beginning of single numbers in the date.

Information Technology Resources – User Guide for Windows 95
© ITR 1999

*Windows' functions*

## How do I ...?

### Change the sounds my computer will play

If you have a sound card and speakers, **press** the 'windows' key or **click** on **'Start'**, **'Settings'**, **'Control Panel'** and **double click** on **'Sounds'** to show this window.  **Scroll** through the 'Events' window and you will see 'Windows' and the sounds it uses for certain events shown below.  **Click** on an event with alongside and the name of its sound file shows in the 'Name' box.  **Click** on ▶ button to hear the sound.  To change it, **click** on the ▼ in the 'Name' box and **click** on another sound.  If you want to see more sound files, **click** on the **'Browse'** button for the sound scheme files and **double click** on the **'Office 97'** folder (if you have one) to see others. **Click** on a sound file and **click** on ▶ button to hear the sound before selecting.

Sound schemes are already set up in Windows, **click** on the ▼ under Schemes to see those you have on your computer.  To add more sound files and schemes to this window, run 'Multimedia' components (see page 64) in Windows setup. Always save your existing scheme by using **'Save As'** before selecting a new scheme.  **Click** on the new scheme and experiment with the sounds it makes. To find out how to play an audio CD on your computer, see page 82.

Information Technology Resources – User Guide for Windows 95
© ITR 1999

79

*Windows' functions*

# How do I ...?

## See the hardware attached to my computer

**Press** the 'windows' ⊞ key or **click** on **'Start'**, **'Settings**, **'Control Panel'** and **double click** on **'System'**. **Click** on the **'Device Manager'** tab to show this window. This shows all the types of 'devices', pieces of 'hardware', that are attached to your computer. **Click** on the 'plus signs' (+) to see more information about each item. **Click** on the + alongside **'Monitor'** and it will show you the type of monitor you are using. **Click** on the 'minus sign' (-) to go back to the original list. Try looking at all the devices and see what is listed.

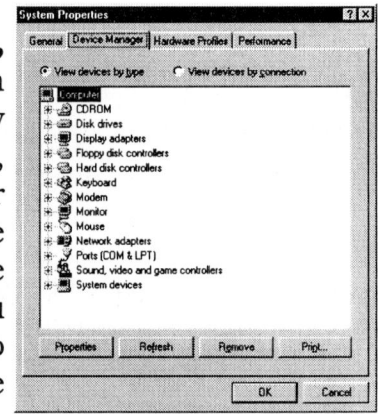

If you 'select' **'Computer'** and **click** on **'Properties'** you will see more details about the 'hardware'.

*Windows' functions*

# How do I ...?

## See how much free space there is on my hard drive

From the desktop, **double click** on **'My Computer'**, **point** at the 'icon' for the disk drive you want to look at, **right click** for the 'shortcut' menu and **click** on **'Properties'** to show this window. Or, **click** on the disk drive and **press 'Alt'** and **'Enter'**.

This shows you the amount of used space and free space on your disk as well as the size of the disk. You can use this for a floppy disk as well as a disk inside your computer. You can see when you last used the 'system tools' (see pages 84-87), that is 'ScanDisk', 'Backup' or 'Defragmenter' in the **'Tools'** tab. Look through the other tabs, yours may not have as many as shown here, to see the settings for 'sharing' and 'compressing' drives. This means you can make more room on your disk.

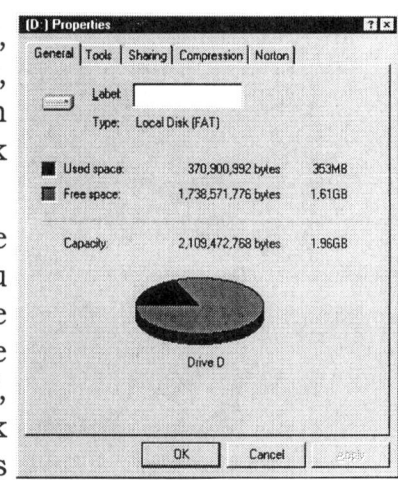

If you are low on disk space and use the internet often, **point** at the 'Internet' icon on the desktop, **press 'Alt'** and **'Enter'**, **click** on **'Navigation'** and **'Clear History'** to delete links to web sites (see also pages 53 and 70).

Information Technology Resources – User Guide for Windows 95
© ITR 1999

81

*Windows' functions*

# How do I ...?

## Play an audio CD on my computer

If you load an audio CD, compact disc, into your computer it will usually start to play automatically, this may take a few moments.  Or, you can **press** the 'windows' key or **click** on **'Start'**, **'Programs'**, **'Accessories'**, **'Multimedia'** and **'CD Player'** to show this window.

You can use the buttons as you would on a CD player or tape recorder to 'Play' (see page 83 to change volume), 'Pause' and 'Stop' the music and 'Eject' the CD.  **Point** to each button and wait for the 'tooltip' to tell you what it does.  The black display tells you which track is playing and how long it has been playing, the length of the track is given at the bottom of the window.  The total play time for the whole CD is also shown.  **Click** on **'Disc'**, **'Edit Play List'** to edit the list of tracks to be played.  **Click** on a track in the 'Available tracks' list, **drag** over its name in the bottom box, **key-in** a new name and **click** on **'Set Name'** and **'OK'** to rename it.  **Click** on **'Options'** to select playing tracks at random or continuously.  Your CD will play even if you 'minimize' the CD Player window.

Information Technology Resources – User Guide for Windows 95
© ITR 1999

*Windows' functions*

# How do I ...?

## Adjust the volume control and record music

You can adjust the volume through your speakers or use the computer's volume control.  **Double click** on the 'Volume' icon in the 'notification area' of the 'taskbar' (see page 20).  Or, you can **press** the 'windows' key or **click** on **'Start'**, **'Programs'**, **'Accessories'**, **'Multimedia'** and **'Volume Control'** to show this window.

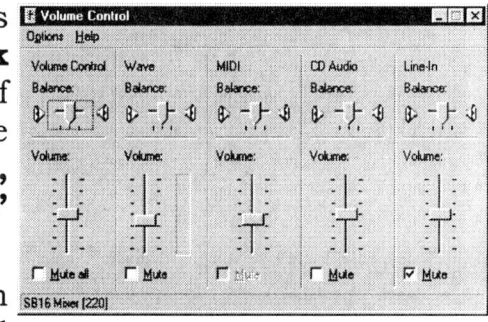

You can **click** on **'Mute all'** to turn off all sound on your computer.  Or, you can adjust the balance and volume for different sound 'devices'.

You can also record from a CD onto your computer.  **Click** on **'Start'**, **'Programs'**, **'Accessories'** **'Multimedia'** and **'Sound Recorder',** start the CD playing and **click** on the **'Record'** button, **click** on **'Stop'** to finish.  You can save the file and play it again.  You can use **'File'**, **'Open'** to recall it.  You can use **'Edit'**, **'Insert File'** to add the same recording, or a different one, into the existing file to make it longer.  If you do not have any of these options, see page 64.

Information Technology Resources – User Guide for Windows 95
© ITR 1999

83

*Windows' functions*

# How do I ...?

## Use system tools

These tools are used to keep your system working at its best. When data is stored on your hard drive (see page 13) it is saved anywhere over the surface of the disk. This can mean that whole files are stored as 'fragments', sections that are not stored together. When you are opening a file, although it opens correctly, it will take longer to find all these 'fragments'. Use 'Disk Defragmenter' to overcome this problem.

**Press** the 'windows' ⊞ key or **click** on 'Start', 'Programs', 'Accessories', 'System Tools' and 'Disk Defragmenter'. You will be asked which disk you want to work on, **drive c:** will be highlighted. **Click** on 'OK' to see this window, and the process will start. You will then be told whether you need to carry out this work. It may take some time, but you will be shown how much of the disk has been worked on. You can use the computer for other things whilst this is running, but it will work more slowly. **Click** on 'Show Details' to see the disk being checked. You should run 'Disk Defragmenter' from time to time.

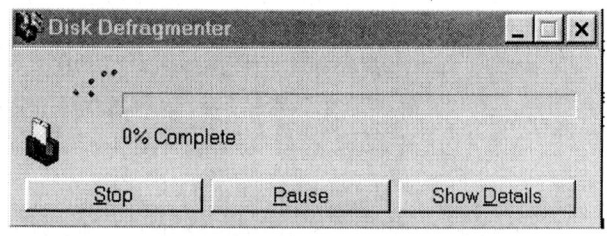

*Windows' functions*

## How do I ...?

### Use ScanDisk

'ScanDisk' is used to check your disks, either the hard drive inside your computer, drive (c:), the 'floppy disk' in drive (a:) or the CD ROM drive (d:).

**Press** the 'windows' ⊞ key or **click** on **'Start'**, **'Programs'**, **'Accessories'**, **'System Tools'** and **'ScanDisk'** to show this window. **'Drive c:'** will usually be selected. You can choose to run a 'Standard' test which will check just files and folders for errors, or you can run 'Thorough'. This will check files and folders as well as checking the surface of the disk for errors or damage. It will also give you further 'Options'. **Click** on **'Automatically fix errors'** and ScanDisk will correct any faults it finds for you. If you do not select this option, you will have to choose how to correct the errors. **Click** on **'Start'**.

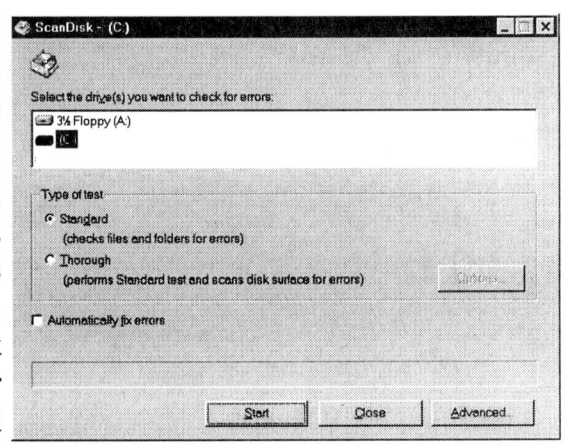

If you are having problems with a disk, it is a good idea to run this program.

Information Technology Resources – User Guide for Windows 95
© ITR 1999

85

*Windows' functions*

# How do I ...?

## Make backup copies of my data

It is vital that you make copies of any important data on your computer. You may have a hard disk failure and be unable to read the information on your disk, which could be lost unless you have a 'backup'. If this program is not on your machine see page 64. **Press** the 'windows' ⊞ key or **click** on **'Start'**, **'Programs'**, **'Accessories'**, **'System Tools'** and **'Backup'** to show a welcome window. You may be reminded that you would only do a full system backup for emergency use, it is more usual just to back up files or folders. You should now see this window.

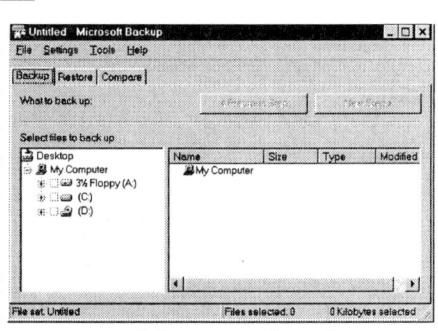

**Click** on the drive which contains the files to be 'backed up'. You will see a list of files and folders. To backup a folder, **click** alongside it and a tick appears, or **click** on separate files. **Click** on **'Next Step>'**. **Click** on the drive where the backup files are to be saved, usually drive a: though you may have a tape device, and **click** on **'Start Backup'**. You will have to name your backup files or 'set'. If there is too much data for one floppy disk, you will be asked to insert another disk. Your file is then given this icon .

*Information Technology Resources – User Guide for Windows 95*
© ITR 1999

*Windows' functions*

# How do I ...?

## Restore backup files

Files which have been 'backed up' can only be read again if they are 'restored'. They are saved in a special format and given a **'.QIC'** file extension (see page 47). **Press** the 'windows' key or **click** on **'Start'**, **'Programs'**, **'Accessories'**, **'System Tools'**, **'Backup'** and **click** on the **'Restore'** tab to show this 'window'.

**Click** on the drive which has the files to be restored, usually drive a:, and the file will show in the right pane of the window. If your files use more than one disk, always put the last disk in first. **Click** on the file to be restored and **click** on **'Next Step'**. **Click** in the box alongside the folder in which your restored file is to be saved and ticks will show your selection. **Click** on **'Start Restore'**. You will be asked to put the first disk into the disk drive if 'backup' used more than one. The files are then restored back to where they came from.

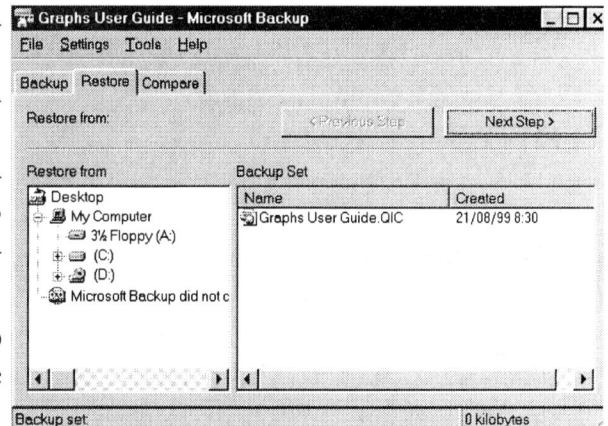

*Windows' functions*

# How do I ...?

## Use the calculator

**Press** the 'windows' ⊞ key or **click** on **'Start'**, **'Programs'**, **'Accessories'**, and **'Calculator'** to show this window.

You can use this on-screen calculator just like you would an ordinary one. You can either **click** on the numbers with the mouse, or **press** the number keys on the keyboard. If you are using the 'Number Pad' (see page 9) check that 'Num Lock' is lit. Use +, -, * and / to add, take away, times and share by. **Click** on '=' to see the result.

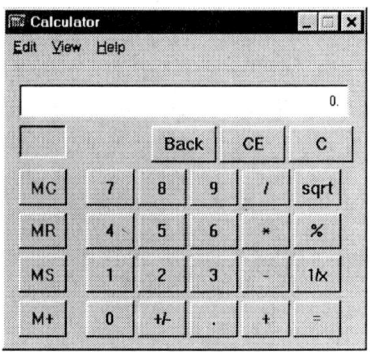

To use the memory function, **click** on **MS** to store a number and an 'M' appears in the box above the memory buttons. To recall a number from memory, **click** on **'MR'**. You can only store one number at a time in the memory. To add the number in the display box to the number in the memory **click** on **'M+'**. To clear the memory, **click** on **'MC'**.

**Click** on **'View'**, **'Scientific'** to make statistical and scientific calculations. To find out what a button does, **click** the right mouse button on it and **click** on **'What's This?'**.

Information Technology Resources – User Guide for Windows 95
© ITR 1999

88

*Windows' functions*

# How do I ...?

## Use HyperTerminal and Dial-up Networking

You can use 'HyperTerminal' to connect your machine to a computer not running 'Windows'. You can dial up the computer's telephone number and find information that is stored there.

However, you would use 'Dial-up Networking' to share information on 2 computers, but one would have to be set up as a network server, that is it must be running Windows NT or another network version of Windows and both computers must have a modem (see page 8). **Press** the 'windows' key or **click** on **'Start'**, **'Programs'**, **'Accessories'** and **'Dial-up Networking'** to see the 'Dial-up Networking' window. **Double click** on **'Make New Connection'** to see the first page of the 'Make New Connection' Wizard. Follow all the instructions and your new connection will then show in the 'Dial-up Networking' window. **Double click** this new 'icon', put in your name and password and **click 'Connect'** to make the call. Useful if you are working at home and want to connect to your office network.

*Windows' functions*

# How do I ...?

## **Scan and change images in Imaging**

Windows provides a program for you to scan pictures, edit them, add text, rotate and flip the images. **Press** the 'windows' ⊞ key or **click** on **'Start'**, **'Programs'**, **'Accessories'** and **'Imaging'** to show this 'window'. If you have a scanner, you can scan a picture straight into this window, **click** on the 'Scan' button. You can save pictures with the file extensions (see page 47) **'.tif'**, **'.awd'** or **'.bmp'**. 'Tif' means 'Tagged Image File Format' and is widely used; good for e-mailing pictures. 'Awd' is a format suitable for faxing. 'Bmp' is a 'bitmap' format which gives larger files than 'Tif'. You can **'Open'** files with other file extensions, but you may not be able to do as much with them.

**Point** to each of the toolbar buttons to see what they do. Experiment with rotating images, using the buttons to move the picture through ¼ circle turns. Or, **click** on **'Page'**, **'Flip'** to move through a ½ circle. **Click** on the 'Annotation Toolbox' button to see another toolbar which lets you add text, shapes, highlighting and even a 'Rubber Stamp' to your picture.

*Windows' functions*

# How do I ...?

## Create, scan and change images in Paint

**Press** the 'windows' ⊞ key or **click 'Start'**, **Programs'**, **'Accessories'** and **'Paint'** to show this window. There are more functions in 'Paint' than in 'Imaging'. You can scan, edit or view picture files or draw new pictures yourself, explore the menus for options. However, you cannot 'Open' as many different types of picture files as you can in 'Imaging'. 'Paint' will only open files with the file extension (see page 47) **'.bmp'** (bitmaps) or files imported from PC Paintbrush with the file extension **'.pcx'**.

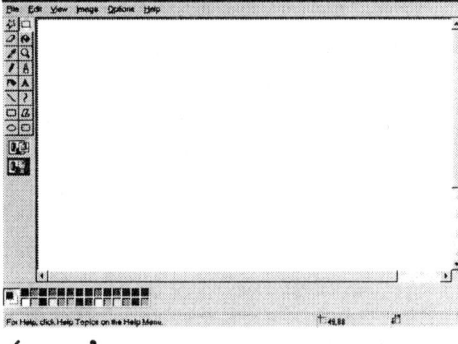

**Click** on the 'Select' button, or **click** on 'Free-form Select' button and the mouse pointer changes to a **+**. **Hold down** the mouse button and **drag** to select an area of a picture. You can then move this part of the image. You can magnify parts of a picture to edit them. You can 'cut', 'copy' and 'paste' (see pages 54 and 55) pictures into other documents. Or, you can save them as 'wallpaper' for your desktop (see page 66). You can draw different lines and shapes and fill them with colour.

*Windows' functions*

# How do I ...?

## Make notes in Windows

**Press** the 'windows' ⊞ key or **click** on **'Start'**, **'Programs'**, **'Accessories'** and **'Notepad'** to show this window. 'Notepad' is a very simple word processing package which can be used for short notes.

You can key-in straight onto this screen. The flashing line is the 'cursor', the point where your text will appear. You do not need to press 'Enter' at the end of a line, **click** on **'Edit'**, **'Word Wrap'** to make the text fit the width of the screen. **Drag** over any text you want to change and **key-in** your new text or, **press 'Delete'** to remove it. To use the 2 delete keys, see page 9. Or, you can **click** on **'Edit'**, **'Cut'** and the text disappears from the screen. **Re-position** the cursor and **click** on **'Edit'**, **'Paste'** to move the text. **Press 'F5'** (function key F5) to add the time and date. Or, **key-in .LOG** on the first line and every time you open the document, 'Notepad' adds the current time and date at the end of the text. For more word processing functions see 'WordPad'.

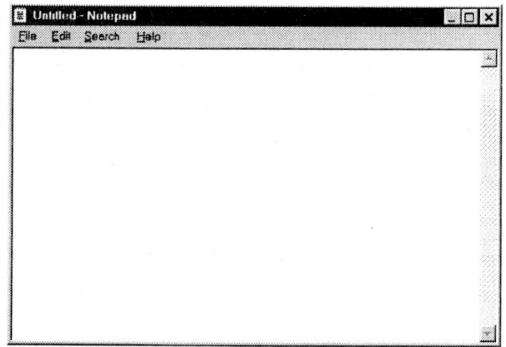

*Windows' functions*

# How do I ...?

## Use WordPad

**Press** the 'windows' ⊞ key or **click** on 'Start', 'Programs', 'Accessories' and 'WordPad' to show this window. 'WordPad' gives you more word processing functions than 'Notepad'. **Point** to each button on the toolbars to see what it will do.

You can 'Print Preview' a document, that is see how it will look when it is printed. Or, you can use 'Find' to search for certain words or phrases. You can 'cut' text out and 'paste' it back into a different place (see page 92), or 'copy' text. **Click** on the 'Undo' ↶ button to reverse (undo) your last action.

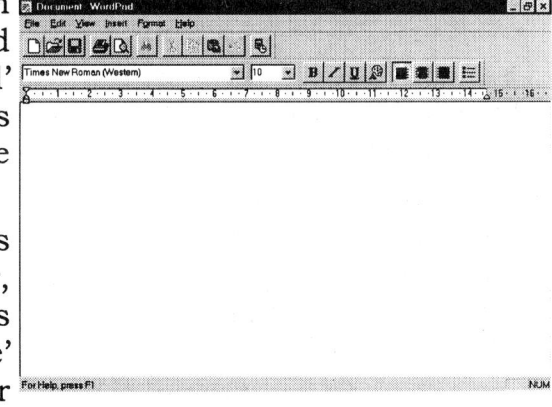

You can change the 'font', that is the style of writing, its size and make it 'bold' - darker print, italic - sloping print, underlined or change the colour. You can change the way the margins look and add 'bullets', dots alongside lines of text to add emphasis. All these functions are on the toolbars. WordPad is useful for writing e-mail letters 'offline' before sending them (see page 110).

*Windows' functions*

# How do I ...?

## Send a fax in Windows

**Click** the right mouse button while pointing to any 'icon' on the desktop, or any file in 'Windows Explorer' (see page 42). **Click** on **'Send To'**, **'Fax Recipient'** to show this window. Or, you can **press** the 'windows' ⊞ key or **click** on **'Start'**, **'Programs'**, **'Accessories'**, **'Fax'** and **'Compose New Fax'** to start the 'Compose New Fax Wizard'.

You will be asked for the name and fax number of the person you are sending the fax to. **Click** on the ▼ in the 'Country' box and **choose** a country and its dialling code. You do not then need to include this number in the telephone code. You will be given a choice of front covers (see page 95). You can then **key-in** your subject heading and message and at the next page you can 'attach' one or more files to be sent with your fax. When you have completed every page of the 'Wizard' **click** on **'Finish'** and watch your fax being sent. If the line is engaged, Windows will try to send it again a few minutes later.

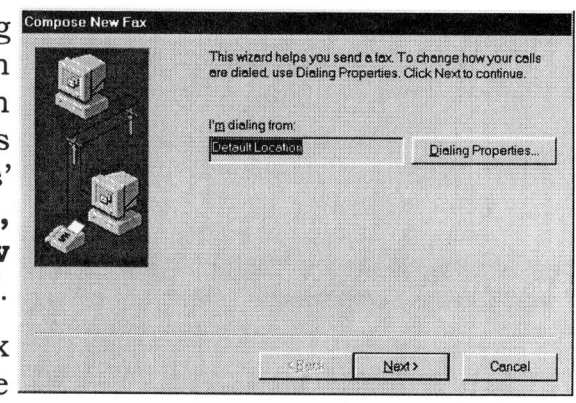

*Wind*

# How do I ...?

## Change my fax cover sheet

**Press** the 'windows' key or **click** on **'Start'**, **'Programs'**, **'Accessories'**, **'Fax'** and **'Cover Page Editor'** to show this 'window'. The 'Cover Page Editor Tips' may be shown, read them and **click** on **'OK'**. There are several cover pages already stored that you can use. These have a 'file extension (see page 47) of **'.cpe'**. **Click** on the 'Open' button. The 'Open' dialogue box' appears, it should show **'Windows'** in the 'Look in:' box. **Scroll** (see page 32) to the end of the file list and you several files which all have the extension **'.cpe'** (though these may shown on your machine – see page 47). **Double click** on one of these see how it will appear when you send a fax.

You can edit the page, **click** on the boxes to 'select' them and when they small, black squares around them called 'handles', **press 'Delete'** to rei the boxes. Or, you can move items to a new place, **select** them and **drag** new position. The information which is put onto this sheet by the compute taken from details you have given it (see page 72).

Information Technology Resources – User Guide for Windows 95
© ITR 1999

*Windows' functions*

# How do I ...?

## Send a scanned page as a fax

If you do not have a separate fax machine, you can scan in a document to be faxed. You can use 'Imaging' or 'Paint' to scan a single document or image. If you have more than one page in the fax, use 'Imaging'. Scan in the last page first then **click** on **'Page', 'Insert', 'Scan Page'** and scan in the next to last page and so on, scanning the first page of the fax last. Each new page is inserted before the one on screen. Once the scan is complete, **click** on **'File', 'Print'** to show this 'dialogue box'. **Click** on the ▼ alongside the 'Name' box which shows the printer you are using. **Click** on **'Microsoft Fax'** and the printer name is changed.

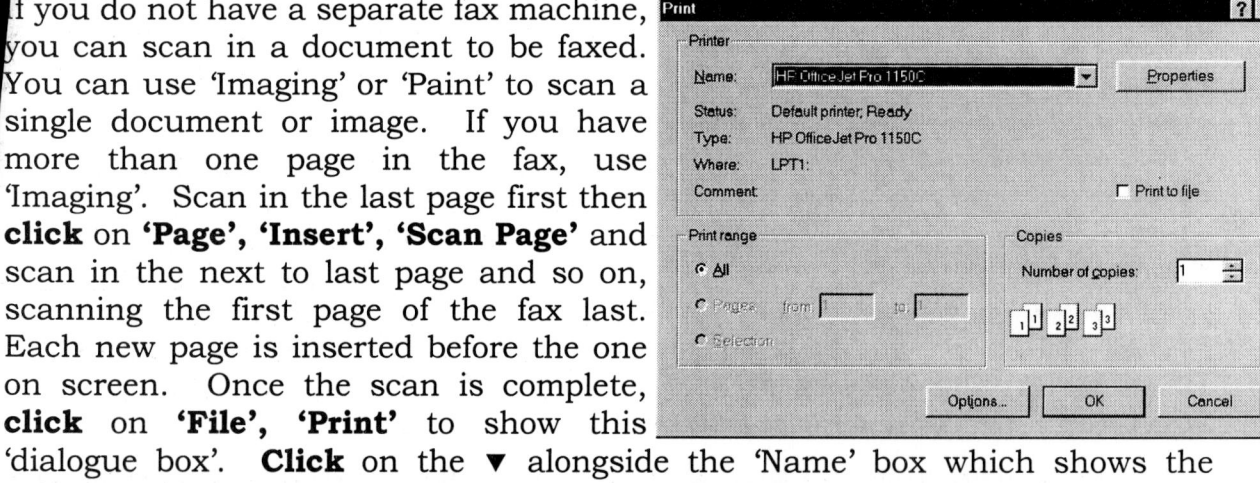

**Click** on **'OK'** to start the 'Compose New Fax Wizard'. Follow the instructions and **click** on **'Finish'** to send your fax.

*Windows' functions*

## How do I ...?

### Receive a fax

You must have 'Microsoft Exchange' running before you can receive a fax. **Double click** on the 'Inbox' icon at the desktop or **press** the 'windows' key or **click** on **'Start'**, **'Programs'**, **'Windows Messaging'**.

If you have a separate telephone line for faxes, you can set up Windows to answer every call. **Press** the 'windows' key or **click** on **'Start'**, **'Settings'**, **'Control Panel'** and **'Mail and Fax'**. Make sure **'Microsoft Fax'** is highlighted and **click** on **'Properties'**. **Click** on the **'Modem'** tab to show this window. **Click** on **'Properties'** to show the 'Fax Modem Properties' window. Under 'Answer mode' **click** on **'Answer after'** and you can then **key-in** the number of rings before the computer answers the telephone call. **Click** on **'OK'**.

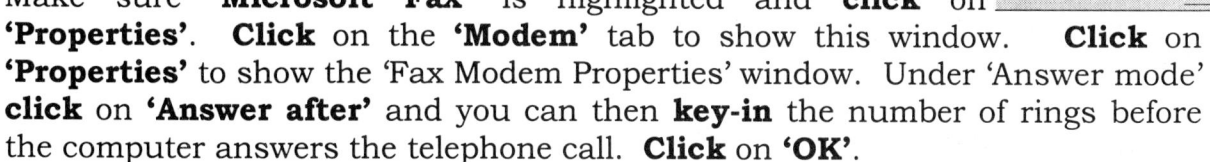

If you want to receive voice calls on your line as well as faxes, under 'Answer mode' **click** on **'Manual'**. When a fax call comes in a screen prompt asks if you want to answer the call, **click** on **'Yes'** to receive the fax. Or, **double click** on the 'Fax' icon in the 'notification area' (see page 20) and **click** on **'Answer Now'**. The fax is then saved in your 'Inbox' in 'Microsoft Exchange'.

*Windows' functions*

# How do I ...?

## **Put a shortcut on my desktop**

You can put shortcuts onto the desktop or into another folder for programs, folders, disk drives, printers or other computers. To add a shortcut for a Microsoft Office 97 program, **open** either **'My Computer'** or **'Windows Explorer'**. **Double click** on **'Program Files'**, **'Microsoft Office'** to see a list of programs. **Click** on the **'Restore'** button (see page 26) until you can see the desktop behind this window. **Click** on a program or **hold down** the 'Ctrl' key and **click** on several programs. **Point** at the highlighting, **hold down** the 'Ctrl' key, 'Shift' key and **drag** onto the desktop and **release** to place the shortcut on the desktop.

If you want to make a shortcut to a program which does not have the icons like Microsoft Office 97, you must look for the file which starts the program. Look for a file with an **'exe'** file extension (see page 47). It will usually include the name or abbreviation for the program. Make a shortcut for this on your desktop. You can delete and rename shortcuts (see page 99).

*Windows' functions*

# How do I ...?

## Edit and arrange shortcut icons on my desktop

**Point** at a shortcut 'icon' and **right click** or **press** 'shortcut' key to see a 'shortcut menu'. You can then delete shortcuts or rename them. If you delete a shortcut this does not delete its program, but it would delete a Windows' function such as 'My Briefcase'. If you delete a program the shortcut stays on the desktop until you remove it.

**Click** on **'Properties'** on this 'shortcut menu' and **click** on **'Shortcut'** to show a window similar to this one. Here you can change the icon for your shortcut, **click** on **'Change Icon'** and make your choice. **Click** on **'OK'**.

To line up the 'icons' on your desktop, **point** to a clear space on the desktop and **click** the right mouse button. **Click** on **'Arrange Icons'** to see this second menu. You can choose **'Auto Arrange'** or you can arrange the icons using the other choices shown. Or, you can **click** and **drag** an 'icon' to move it to a different place, but you must first take off 'Auto Arrange', **click** on it to remove the tick, before you can drag the 'icons'.

Information Technology Resources – User Guide for Windows 95
© ITR 1999

99

*Windows' functions*

## How do I ...?

### Add a program to the Start menu

If you want to add, for example, the 'Paint' program which is found in 'Accessories' to your 'Start' menu, **open 'My Computer'** or **'Windows Explorer'**. **Double click** on **'C:'**, **'Program Files'**, **'Accessories'** to see this 'window'. **Click** with the left mouse button on **'Mspaint.exe'** and **drag** the 'icon' down until it is over the 'Start' button on the taskbar. Let go of the mouse button and **click** on **'Start'** to see that this program has now been added to the start menu.

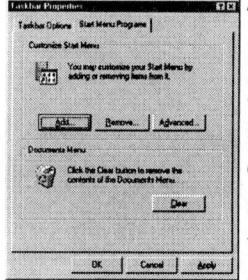

To remove an item from the 'Start' menu, **press** the 'windows' key or **click** on **'Start', 'Settings', 'Taskbar'** and **'Start Menu Programs'** to show this window. **Click** on **'Remove'** to see a list of shortcuts in 'Programs', this is the list that shows when you **click** on **'Start', 'Programs'**. At the bottom of the list are items that show at the top of the menu when you **click** on **'Start'**. **Click** on the 'shortcut' to be deleted, **click** on **'Remove'**, confirm the deletion, **'Close'** and **'OK'**. You can add items to the 'Start' menu this way, or clear the files that show when you **press 'Start', 'Documents'**.

Information Technology Resources – User Guide for Windows 95
© ITR 1999

*Windows' functions*

## How do I ...?

### Load a program onto the desktop when Windows starts

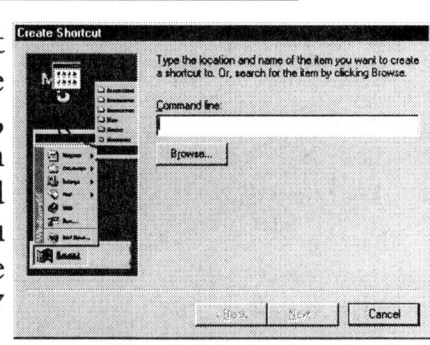

If is quicker to have the programs you use the most opening at the same time as Windows. **Press** the 'windows' ⊞ key or **click** on **'Start'**, **'Settings'**, **'Taskbar'** and **'Start Menu Programs'**. **Click** on **'Add'** to show this window. **Click** on **'Browse'** to find the program. Look in the **'Program Files'** folder, you may need to **click** on the horizontal scroll bar (see page 32), and **'Microsoft Office'** for Office 97 programs. Or, from **'Program Files'** look in the **'Accessories'** folder for the 'Paint' or 'WordPad' program to find the **'.exe'** file which runs that program. **Double click** to make your choice.

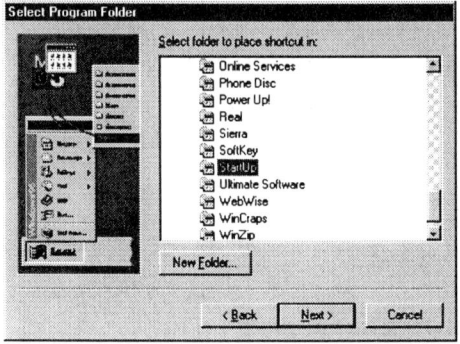

**Click** on **'Next'** to show this window. **Scroll** down the list and **click** on **'StartUp'**. **Click** on **'Next'** and **'Finish'**. **Click** on **'OK'**. Your chosen program will now load onto the 'desktop' every time Windows starts.

*Windows' functions*

## How do I ...?

### Load a program onto the taskbar when Windows starts

If you are opening several programs with Windows, it might be better to open all or some of these windows minimized.  **Open 'Windows Explorer'. Double click** on **'C:', 'Windows', 'Start Menu', 'Programs', 'StartUp'** folder.  **Click** with the right mouse button on the program shortcut you wish to minimize to the taskbar, **click** on **'Properties'** and the **'Shortcut'** tab to show this window.

Do not minimize the program you use the most.  For other programs **click** on the ▼ alongside 'Run' and **click** on **'Minimized'** for any programs you want to show on the taskbar.  **Click** on **'OK'**.  **Restart** your computer and the program or programs will appear on the taskbar.  If you find problems with running all these programs at the same time (see page 35) you can remove them, **right click** on the program in the **'StartUp'** folder and **press 'Delete'**.

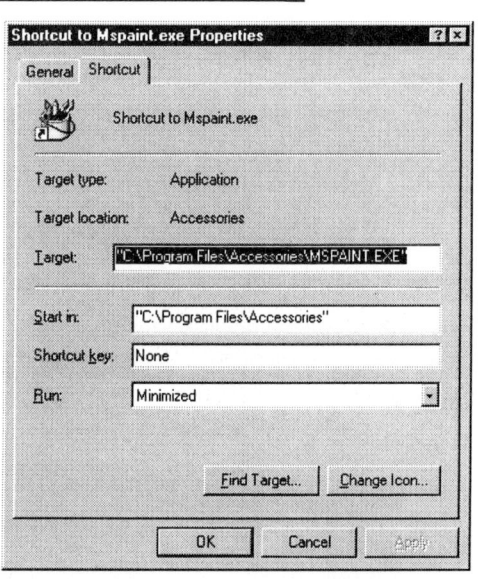

*Windows' functions*

## How do I ...?

### Run a program

Most programs will now run from a CD as soon as this is put into the disk drive. However, you may need to run a program which is not a 'shortcut' on your desktop, or listed in 'Programs' on your 'Start' menu.

**Insert** the CD or disk and **press** the 'windows' key and **'r'** or **click** on **'Start'**, **'Run'** to show this window. The file in the 'Open' box will be from the drive where you have put the CD or disk. If this is not the file you want, **click** on **'Browse'** to show this second window, although everyone's will look slightly different. **Click** on the file you want, this will be **'Setup.exe'** if you are wanting to load the program onto your computer, or a file with a **'.exe'** file extension to start the program itself. **Click** on **'Open'** and **'OK'**.

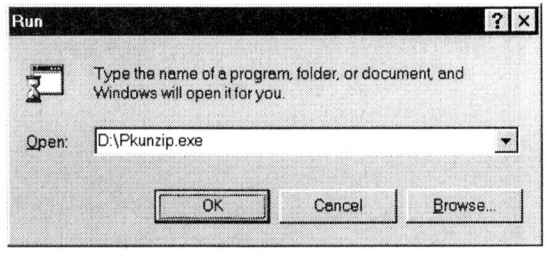

*Windows' functions*

# How do I ...?

## Share folders and printers

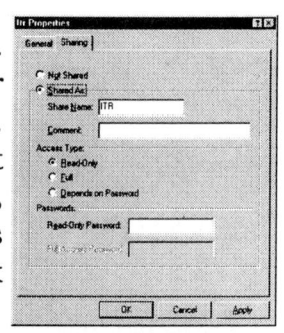

You can share things when you are connected to a network. You could use 'Dial-Up Networking' to connect your computer to another and then share folders stored on that computer. **Open 'Windows Explorer'** and find the folder that you want to share. **Point** to it and **right click, click** on **'Sharing'** from the 'shortcut menu'. If this item is not on your menu, see your Network Administrator who will install file sharing for you. At the 'Properties' window the 'title bar' shows the name of the folder. **Click** on the 'Sharing' tab to show this 'window'. **Click** on **'Shared As'** and **click** on the type of access your sharer will have. **Click** on **'OK'**. Your folder now has this new icon.

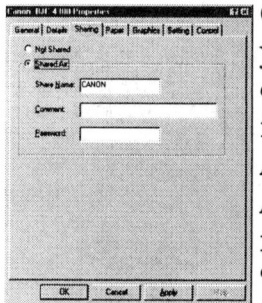

**Press** the 'windows' key or **click** on **'Start'**, **'Settings'**, **'Printers'** and **click** on the printer to share. **Click** on **'File'**, **'Sharing'** and **click** on the 'Sharing' tab to see this 'window'. **Click** on **'Shared As'** and **'OK'**. Your printer's icon in the printer folder now has a hand shown on the bottom of the logo. This hand shows this is a shared resource.

Information Technology Resources – User Guide for Windows 95
© ITR 1999

*Windows' functions*

## How do I ...?

### Connect to the internet

You will need a telephone line, 'modem' and an Internet Service Provider (ISP) (see page 17) before you can get onto the internet.  Follow the instructions given with the CD ROM or disk to load the 'software' for your ISP.  You will have to set up a 'user name', 'password' and an e-mail address which people will use to send messages to you (see page 110).

When you have finished all the installation, **double click** on **'The Internet'** icon at the 'desktop' or **double click** on your ISP's icon.  Some ISP's cannot be loaded through **'The Internet'** icon.  For those that can, you will see a window which looks something like this.  You will have to **key-in** your password, remember this will show as a line of stars (*) (see page 75) and you can then load the software which will connect you to the internet.  You can change your connection at any time, **press** the 'windows' key or **click** on **'Start'**, **'Programs'**, **'Accessories'**, **Internet Tools'** and **'Get on the Internet'** to open the 'Internet Connection Wizard' and make your changes.

*Windows' functions*

# How do I ...?

## Use the internet

When you connect to the internet, this is called 'logging-on', you will see the 'home page' of your Internet Service Provider. Everyone's will look different. This shows an example of the type of screen you will see. There are 'menus' and 'toolbars' (see page 44) which you can **point to** and see what each button does. There is a box, or you may have to **click** on **'Address'** to see this, which has lots of letters, dots and forward slashes (/) in it and it begins with **'http://'**. This is the 'Universal Resource Locator' or **'URL'**, which means it is an address which will take you to that page on the web (see page 17). All URL's begin with **http://** (this means 'Hypertext Transmission Protocol', the language computers use to send and receive files on the web).

The 'toolbar' has 2 very useful buttons, **'Back'** and **'Stop'**. These will take you back to the previous page, or stop a long page loading. You can print pages straight from the web, or **select** information you want and **'Cut and paste'** it into a word processing package (see page 110).

*Windows' functions*

## How do I ...?

### Visit a web page if I know the address

**Double click** on your ISP's (see page 17) icon, or **press** the 'windows' ⊞ key or **click** on **'Start' 'Programs'** and **click** on your ISP's name from the menu. **Key-in** your 'password', or you can store this so you do not have to give it every time, and your ISP will then load a 'browser'. This is special 'software' which lets you move through the different pages and sites on the world wide web. Two browsers are 'Microsoft Internet Explorer' and 'Netscape Communicator'.

**Click** on the place on your screen where you **key-in** the address of the site (see page 106) and **key-in**, for example, www.it-resources.co.uk to see ITR's web page. All addresses begin with **'http://'** so you do not need to key this in. You should always use small letters. The computer will then find the page you asked for. For ITR you will have to **click** on the logo to see the 'home page', the opening page of the site. When you **point** to words in blue with a line underneath and the mouse pointer becomes a flat hand, this is a 'link', **click** on it to go to another page or site. Once you have clicked on a link it changes colour. **Click** on the **'Back'** ⇦ button to go back to the last page. Experiment with moving through the different pages and **click** on **'Alt F4'** or the 'Close' ✕ button to leave the internet.

*Windows' functions*

# How do I ...?

## Search for information on the world wide web

**Load** your ISP (see page 105).  All the ISPs' home pages will look different, but they will all have their own 'Search' function which will look something like this example from Netscape Online.
**Click** in the 'Search the web' box and **key-in** a word or words to search for, **click** on ▼ alongside **'UK Plus'** to see other 'search engines' you can choose and **click** on **'go'**.  'Search engines' help you find the information you want.  There are lots of different ones, 'AltaVista' and 'HotBot' search the entire web for words which match the ones you key-in.  'Yahoo' and 'Excite' look for categories or locations.  'Yell' and 'Bigfoot' find telephone numbers and e-mail addresses.  If you want to choose a different 'search engine', you can **key-in** its address (see page 106)**,** for example, **'www.lycos.co.uk'** to go to the 'home page' of 'Lycos'.

When you key-in words to search for, try to use words which will bring the answers you want.  For example, **'york'** would find thousands of pages to look through.  **Key-in 'york+dungeon'** and **click** on **'go'**.  This will limit your search and only find information which applies to both the words.  You cannot use the plus sign (+) with all search engines, some require a space.

*Windows' functions*

# How do I ...?

## Understand e-mail addresses

E-mail (see page 17) addresses are always keyed-in in small letters and begin with a name that you give yourself, sometimes this may include 'underscores' (_), 'hyphens' (-) or numbers. Then there is an **@,** the 'at' sign, and the 'domain' name. The 'domain' name is usually the name of your ISP, such as **'freeserve'** or **'aol'**. However, you can buy your own 'domain' name from the internet society, just like you buy a personal car registration number. The 'domain' name is followed by a dot '.' and letters such as these.

| .com | Used by businesses in the United States of America |
| --- | --- |
| .co | Used by companies |
| .org | Used by non-profit making organisations |
| .ac | Use by universities in the United Kingdom |
| .sch | Used by schools in the United Kingdom |
| .gov | Used by Governments |

For addresses outside America, there can then be another dot '.' and letters to show which country the computer is in, such as **'uk'** for 'United Kingdom' or **'jp'** for 'Japan'.

*Windows' functions*

# How do I ...?

## Send e-mail through the internet

To keep down costs, it is a good idea to **key-in** your message in a word processing package, **select** it by **dragging** over it with the mouse and it turns black, **click** on '**Edit**', '**Copy**'. Go 'online' by **loading** your ISP (see page 105) or e-mail software. **Click** on '**mail**' and **click** on '**Compose**' or '**Write new mail**'. A screen something like this will appear. You must **key-in** the e-mail address (see page 109) of the person it is going to alongside '**To**'. If you want to send a copy to another person, **key-in** their e-mail address alongside '**cc**' (carbon copy). If you want to send a copy to a third person without the second person knowing they too have had a copy, **key-in** an address alongside '**bcc**' (blind carbon copy). To add a file such as a scanned photograph or picture, **click** on '**Attachment**', find the file and **click** on it. You must **key-in** a heading alongside '**Subject**'. When you want to enter your message, **hold down** the 'Ctrl' key and **press v** to paste your message in. **Click** on '**Send**'. You can then '**Close**' your ISP program and this is called coming 'offline'.

*Windows' functions*

# How do I ...?

## Use an Address Book

You can keep a list of e-mail addresses of the people you often write to in your 'Address Book'. Then when you send them a message, you do not have to key-in their address every time.

This window shows an example of a 'new card' in your 'Address Book'. These will be slightly different in each software. **Key-in** all the details, using the 'Tab' key to move from one box to the next and then **click** on **'OK'**. When you are writing your e-mail, **click** in the 'To' box and **click** on the 'Address Book'. Find the address of the person you are writing to and **double click** on it to add it to your e-mail message.

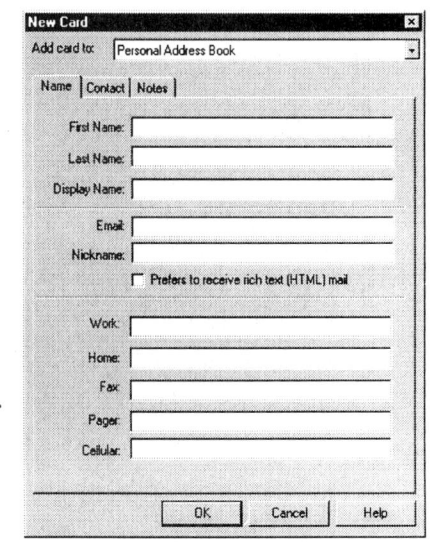